BUILDING THE BENEDICT OPTION

LEAH LIBRESCO

Building the Benedict Option

A Guide to Gathering Two or Three Together in His Name

IGNATIUS PRESS   SAN FRANCISCO

Cover images
Little Houses
Shutterstock/Katsiaryna Yudo
Monstrance
www.holyart.fr

Cover design and stitching by Davin Carlson

© 2018 by Ignatius Press, San Francisco
All rights reserved
ISBN 978-1-62164-217-6
Library of Congress Control Number 2018931247
Printed in the United States of America ∞

For everyone who has eaten in my home or fed me in theirs
and for Alexi, who cooks things up with me

CONTENTS

FOREWORD

Benedictine monasteries have priors and abbots. Benedictine lay communities have den mothers—or ought to.
Leah Libresco is the den mother of the Benedict Option.

I knew this from the moment I met her. Though we did
not know each other aside from e-mails, Leah made me
feel instantly at ease. By the end of the evening, I was convinced of two things: Leah is one of the sharpest intellectual
Catholics I know, and she loves people more than ideas.

In the often-bruising world of Christian apologetics and
public debate, that is a rare and beautiful thing, a something worth celebrating, cherishing, and passing on.

Leah Libresco has a special gift for hospitality, that
most Benedictine of charisms. This became clear to me
when I interviewed her for *The Benedict Option*. Listening to Leah tell me how she organized Benedict Option
events in Washington, D.C., where she lived at the time,
I thought that all of this seems so obviously the right and
natural thing to do, but so few people do it. In the early
1990s, as a young Catholic professional living in D.C., I
was deeply lonely in the faith and longed for connection
to other believers, especially fellow single Catholics living
so far from our homes in a new city. As Leah and I spoke,
I thought about what a difference a Leah Libresco would
have made in my life as a Catholic back then.

The amazing thing about Leah's way is that it is so ordinary, so achievable. Like the Rule of Saint Benedict, Leah's
wisdom is of the everyday kind, a sort so plain that it's easy

9

to overlook. To read this book is not just to encounter good ideas, but also to awaken to one's own gifts for hospitality and community-building.

True story: Last Sunday at coffee hour at my church, I found myself talking to three people who were new in the parish and had become catechumens. I wished I could spend more time with them, but I thought about how busy my family's weekends usually are, how much work it would be to have a dinner party, and how these folks—a young couple with a toddler and a single man—probably had plans anyway.

Then it hit me: "What would Leah Libresco do?" Having just finished reading this book, I applied Leah's advice. I was overthinking the matter. I didn't have to stage a fancy dinner. The point was to get us all around the same table to share a meal, drink some wine, tell stories, and become better friends. Keep it simple. Focus on the people.

After clearing it with my wife, I invited the catechumens to come over on Saturday night. Their faces lit up. *Yes*, they all said, enthusiastically. Turns out they had been hoping someone would invite them over sometime. We also learned in that conversation that the young couple had been desperate to find a babysitter for their toddler, because they hadn't had a night out alone since he was born. My wife and our three kids love to babysit.

Just like that, our little mission parish became a little less a group of people who go to church together, and a little more of a community, indeed a family. It's a small thing, but it's everything. And I would not have found the courage to make that small step if it had not been for the graces in the little book you hold in your hands.

This is what Leah Libresco can do for you. This is what Leah Libresco can do for your community. This is what Leah Libresco can do for the Church.

It shouldn't be the case that people have to relearn what it means to be Christians in community, but we do. We didn't make this world of alienation and fragmentation, but it's our responsibility to repair the brokenness wherever we can. This is why *Building the Benedict Option* is so valuable. It's not a book of abstract theorizing, but rather a book of applied Christianity. It's exactly the kind of thing I was hoping that my book *The Benedict Option* would engender: imaginative responses from other Christians who bring their distinct gifts to our common project.

Leah's apostolate is an excellent example of what Pope Benedict XVI meant when he called on believers living in the post-Christian West to see themselves and to act as a "creative minority". The Church today does not lack for diagnosticians who can tell you what's wrong with the world. What it needs is joy-filled believers who see the crisis for what it is, but who also see what we caught up in it can become, if we try. What it needs are Christians who can see that the world is still, as Russell Kirk said, "sunlit despite its vices".

What the world needs is more Leah Libresco. Read this book. You'll see. Read it with your friends. It'll change your life.

Rod Dreher
Baton Rouge, Louisiana

I

Accidental Stylites

I've never felt called to imitate Saint Simeon Stylites. I've never sensed God calling me to build a pillar on top of a tower or a mountain and to live an ascetic life on it, far from other people. But God doesn't need to call stylites anymore. It's easy to become one accidentally.

Although marriage and monasticism would both require me to seek out someone else—husband or mother superior—to discern with and to guide me, the atomized nature of modern life makes it possible to become a hermit unintentionally. This situation is a big departure from the history of hermits. At the time of the Desert Fathers, a monk who wanted to live alone had to get the permission of his spiritual father, because living alone, just he and God, was not something to undertake lightly. It was an unusual calling that required exceptional spiritual discipline. Living one's faith alone, without preparation, is the religious equivalent of trying to run a marathon without so much as a jogging habit as preparation.

As a convert from atheism, I didn't grow up in a Christian family with Christian traditions, so, when I came into the Church, I knew how badly I needed friends and mentors to depend on as I learned how to live as a Catholic. Fortunately, I had Catholic college friends and Dominican friars who talked to me and introduced me to other twenty-something Catholics they knew. This thick community helped me to begin my new life and, just as importantly, helped me to sustain it.

My need was obvious to everyone who knew that I was a convert, but I found that a number of my Christian friends longed for more of a community, for more opportunities to pray with others, for all the things that everyone had hurried to give me as a new Christian. But cradle Catholics don't always know how to ask for these things or whom to ask for them.

And the problem seemed to be bigger than just my parish. Rod Dreher, an Orthodox layman, on his blog and in his book *The Benedict Option*, speaks of a crisis of lonely American Christians. He took the name of his book and his project of community creation from the final pages of Alasdair MacIntyre's work of moral philosophy *After Virtue*.

MacIntyre wrote that moral philosophy had regressed as a discipline and that philosophers' reluctance to think teleologically—to think about everything as having natural aims and characters—doomed moral philosophy to incoherence and irrelevance. Hence, he felt the need for a sort of Saint Benedict, who could stand against this muddled ideology, not by opposing it directly in debate but by building something different, whose virtues would themselves be a rebuke to these pale errors. MacIntyre wrote, "What matters at this stage is the construction of local forms of community within which civility and the intellectual and moral life can be sustained through the new dark ages which are already upon us.... We are waiting not for a Godot, but for another—doubtless very different—St. Benedict."[1]

The specific trait that MacIntyre admired about Benedict and his monks was their independence from worldly

---

[1] Alasdair MacIntyre, *After Virtue*, 3rd ed. (Notre Dame: University of Notre Dame Press, 2007), 263.

institutions and culture. When he described what he hoped his readers would imitate in Saint Benedict, he wrote:

> A crucial turning point in that earlier history occurred when men and women of goodwill turned aside from the task of shoring up the Roman imperium and ceased to identify the continuation of civility and moral community with the maintenance of that imperium. What they set themselves to achieve instead—often not recognizing fully what they were doing—was the construction of new forms of community within which the moral life could be sustained.[2]

In Saint Benedict's case, his influence went beyond his monasteries. Villages in the shadow of the monasteries were sustained by the monks' prayer and work. As a young Catholic living in Washington, D.C., I was blessed to stand in the intersection of a different order of friars and the secular world.

The parish where I was baptized had two Dominican friars who assisted at Mass and ran an adult Sunday school, where they taught the faith to anyone who wanted to learn more about it. One of these Dominicans became my godfather. The Dominicans organized lectures, both at their priory and in the living rooms of their friends. One year, when my office adopted summer hours and let us out early on Fridays, I was able to take the subway to the Dominican House of Studies to pray Evening Prayer with the friars and anyone else who stopped in. My first date with the man I would eventually marry was a trip to the priory to celebrate the Vigil of All Saints.

The Dominicans carved out the same kind of space in the middle of a city that the Benedictines did for their villages. They strengthened everyone in their orbit, through

---

[2] Ibid.

their total gift of self to God, to love each other and to go out and share the reason for their hope. I suggested to one of my college friends, when he was choosing between internships, that he should spend a summer in D.C. I wanted him to share the community I had found with the Dominicans so that he could decide, as he went through law school, whether that sort of community was something he wanted in his life and whether satisfying that desire would shape his career choices.

For laymen, the Benedict Option described by Dreher is finding a way to live in the intersection of the monastery and the world. In some cases, there may already be a nearby group of friendly Dominicans (or Benedictines or Franciscans or Sisters of Life) to attach oneself to, but, as I've moved for jobs and other reasons, I haven't always been as lucky as I was in D.C.

Building the Benedict Option requires me to find a way to root myself in the faith, to connect myself to something larger than myself. I know I'm not ready to live a stylite's existence, sustained only by individual prayer; I need spiritual training wheels. I need more living examples of the Christian life who aren't tucked away in stories of saints; I'm in too much danger of closing the book and leaving them behind.

Thick communities make it easier for me to be confronted. They give me what Stephen Sondheim's Bobby pleads for at the end of the musical *Company*:

> Somebody need me too much.
> Somebody know me too well.
> Somebody pull me up short,
> And put me through hell,
> And give me support
> For being alive.[3]

---

[3] Stephen Sondheim, "Being Alive", in George Furth, *Company* (1970).

ACCIDENTAL STYLITES

17

This kind of support is harder to find in our modern culture these days, when many of us don't have extended families, passels of siblings, or lively neighborhoods full of people who find it natural to be interested in and entangled with each other's lives.

Eve Tushnet, a Catholic who often writes on sexuality and friendship, observes that married people and vowed religious have a kind of responsibility to others that single people, especially single people living alone, can miss. She recommends living with someone, whenever you can, to avoid the challenge of being your own abbot. She writes, "The abbot isn't just a spiritual director, whom you may obey but whom you can also get away from. You live with your abbot; he's inescapable. So spouses can mutually abbot one another, and celibate partners could abbot one another; life in a family household could provide abboting for a celibate layperson."[4]

To imitate the generosity of the Dominicans (and the character of many of the friends I met through them), I've tried to open my house and change the way I plan my social and spiritual life, to save myself and my friends from the loneliness of self-abboting. My goal, always, in building the Benedict Option, is not to turn away from the world but to awake my faith, so that I might live a more Christian life at home and in the world.

Some commenters who are skeptical of the Benedict Option (as Dreher describes it) worry that it is a temptation to build inappropriately cloistered communities. Feeling the need for the thicker community of the Benedict Option, however, isn't the same as rejecting the world or fearing it. It's easy to wind up feeling as if you're living

[4] Eve Tushnet, "'Gay in Christ: Dimensions of Fidelity': Notes from Day One", *Patheos*, October 31, 2014, http://www.patheos.com/blogs/evetushnet/2014/10/gay-in-christ-dimensions-of-fidelity-notes-from-day-one.html.

the faith in a defensive crouch without ever having been pressed to resist sin to the point of shedding blood (see Heb 12:4) or even just to the point of answering awkward questions about why you're a Christian. A claustrophobic feeling can creep into your spiritual life when you practice it alone.

Before I started making a deliberate effort to pray with others, I slipped into the default of praying only in church and in the privacy of my home. I was so nervous about inadvertently giving offense among my religiously mixed friends and family that I crossed myself under the table at meals (or in the kitchen ahead of time), lest I be seen saying grace.

Other people could sometimes call God-talk out of me, if they asked me about the Church's position on a hot-button issue or about why I converted, but these conversations didn't really have the open, joyful character that I hoped for. When my non-Christian friends pick the lens through which we examine the faith, they seldom choose one that focuses on the heart of my faith. Even when they ask with the best of intentions, I wind up discussing something at the margins or some consequence of my belief, without ever getting the chance to share the reason for my hope.

It's hard for any relationship, with God or with anyone else, to flourish under such conditions. Imagine having a really close friend or a spouse whom you never saw or mentioned in public. Such secrecy would have to be a deliberate choice, because it is natural to share our joy with our friend and to share our joy in our friend with others. I've always been prone to blurt out my delight, whether it's sparked by the baby picture a friend has just sent, an interesting fact in an article I've just read, or my happiness in seeing my husband in the morning (he, of course, is often on the receiving end of all my exclamations).

It's strange for God alone to be a private joy. The work of suppressing our joy in Him engenders shame in us. For me, to keep my faith secret and private feels a little like lying. I may not be actively telling untruths, but keeping silent, keeping my rosary in my purse on the subway, makes me feel as if I'm pretending I live in a different world, one where God isn't with me and I'm not Catholic. It's not that I want to proselytize everyone I meet or to talk about my faith all the time. What I want is to find myself more often in the atmosphere of the coffee hour after Mass at my parish. That church basement, full of parents chasing children who are messily eating donuts, is a space in which it feels natural to ask a friend (or even a stranger) about which saint's medal she is wearing and what drew her to that saint. There, it is a little easier than usual to ask someone to pray for me.

I want social spaces that will give me that sort of breathing room a little more often—places where it feels natural to talk about my faith without worrying that it will be a prelude to an argument about apologetics or a kind of anti-evangelization if I ended up talking about it wrong.

But, if we look back to the original evangelizers, we see that the apostles also took time to be with God—alone and with others. My friend Bryce pointed out that in the Gospel of Matthew, we hear a little more about what it means to be fishers of men. In a message to a group I belong to, Bryce said, "If fishing is a metaphor for the Church's work ('I will make you fishers of men'), it's noteworthy that we see the Apostles not only 'casting a net' (4:18) but also 'mending their nets' (4:21). If casting represents preaching, spreading the gospel, suffering martyrdom, etc., what does mending represent? In any case, it alerts us to the fact that spreading the gospel is going to be rough: there will be damages."

The Benedict Option is a way to mend nets and to prepare to cast them out again. Trying to thicken my community and open my home gives me the chance to live my faith more openly and more truthfully.

That faith, rooted in Jesus Christ, is the same yesterday, today, and forever. The Benedict Option doesn't involve any major theological discoveries or startling new spiritual gifts. In my life, and in this book, the most powerful tools I've found are simple: inviting friends over for dinner and praying the Divine Office, giving friends looking for work a chance to pray together (and to proofread cover letters), hosting a night of poetry recitation at a time when my friends and I felt starved for beauty.

I hope that, when reading this book, you put it down frequently, in order to start planning small events of your own. The tools I've relied on (scheduling software for coordinating groups, cooking plans to feed large crowds, seating tricks to help people feel at home) all require almost nothing but a hunger for hospitality and a willingness to be the first one to open your home in this way to your friends.

Some Benedict Option initiatives take place over the long term. There are groups founding classical schools, trying to coordinate moves for members to live in the same town or on the same block, or working out more formal rules of prayer and communal life for laymen. In this book, I will cover only what you can do in the next month or, more often, in the next week, so that, whatever long-term plans or hopes you have, you can start building the community that will sustain them and, more importantly, you.

Now is a very acceptable time.

2

Enemies of the Benedict Option

When the outside world starts to pinch Christian practice, it's tempting to look for a way to fight back. After all, as C. S. Lewis writes in *Mere Christianity*, Christians are always exiles, always fighters in a resistance. Lewis writes, "Enemy-occupied territory—that is what this world is. Christianity is the story of how the rightful king has landed, you might say landed in disguise, and is calling us all to take part in a great campaign of sabotage. When you go to church you are really listening-in to the secret wireless from our friends. that is why the enemy is so anxious to prevent us from going."[1]

But when we find our Enemy in our non-Christian neighbors, we're setting our sights too low. Paul writes in his Letter to the Ephesians, "We wrestle not against flesh and blood, but against principalities, against powers" (Eph 6:12, KJV). The Enemy that Lewis refers to isn't an earthly enemy—although he can be served by humans and human institutions. Paul and Lewis mean for us to arm ourselves against the devil, and we fool ourselves when we try to pick a different fight.

We are fighting *for* the whole world, acting like Radio Liberty operators to rally the rest of our occupied brethren.

---

[1] C. S. Lewis, *The Complete C. S. Lewis Signature Classics* (New York: Harper-One, 2002), 46.

We are called to be channels of grace, letting the kingdom pierce and heal our present, passing world. Our acts of resistance may include conventional political action, but they are usually subtler and more personal—which is often true of political resistance as well.

In 1944, the Office of Strategic Services (OSS) created the *Simple Sabotage Field Manual*, intending to distribute it to allies in danger of Nazi occupation. The guide is no *Anarchist's Cookbook*; instead of instructing civilians in bomb making, the book sternly warns the aspiring saboteur not to overreach. If you've never worked with explosives, the author warns, now is not the moment to let your romantic notions of rebellion carry you away. The goal of the book is to give any reader *something* to do to frustrate the occupying forces. For most people, creating small snags is a better plan that engineering violent and dramatic ones.

The spy-written handbooks advise the reader to leave tools in the wrong place, to clog any machines he can reach (toilets included), and to hamper decisions by referring them to committees. The sort of Christian resistance that Lewis envisions consists of actions just as humble, though considerably pleasanter. The OSS's pupil is meant to seize every feasible opportunity, trusting that a thousand small acts of resistance will add up, instead of sitting on his hands, waiting for one big chance to act. Christians, too, should be panting (like the deer for running streams of Psalm 42) to offer any small act for the glory of God. Holding the door for an arthritic stranger, quietly praying for each person in your line of sight on a train or a bus, e-mailing a photo of a sacred artwork to a friend—each of these small things, done for God, becomes one strand in a tapestry of praise.

The most serious enemies of the Benedict Option and of Christian life are those that strike at our ability and our desire to serve each other. Whether they devalue love, steal our time, or prevent us from putting down roots, they bear the same wicked fruit. They deceive us about our true vocation: to be like Christ, offering sacrificial love to our neighbor.

Facing Down the Enemy Within

Thinking too much about the Benedict in the Benedict Option can lead both critics and fans of Rod Dreher's project into error. Dreher and MacIntyre praise Benedict for his responsiveness to the pressures of his time, for offering a shelter for the faithful and a witness to those who were struggling or fallen away. It is this that BenOp Christians should try to imitate, not necessarily his world-historical role. Nor is it necessary for laymen and families to conform themselves to Benedict's Rule for monks—we have already been given the most important rule for our lives; everything else is a supplement.

We long to correct ourselves through many small rules because we struggle to apply the two great rules that Christ said comprised all the commandments: "Love the Lord your God with all your heart, and with all your soul, and with all your mind, and with all your strength" and "Love your neighbor as yourself" (Mk 12:30–31).

The closer we draw to God and the more we conform our will to His, the easier it is to follow those two rules. They are, after all, the rules we were made for. To act in any other way strains us, like a spring stretched beyond its tensile strength. But sin and past habits of sin make it hard to trust our intellects and wills. When we receive general precepts, we begin looking for loopholes or subtle, almost-plausible opportunities to misinterpret Christ's words. We do better to look to the saints and the rules they set down for living so that we can restrain our unruly desires and pattern our consciences on their holy example. Still, the ultimate goal isn't to follow any other person's rule of life, even Saint Benedict's, for its own sake, but to use it to grow in love for and obedience to God.

Ross Douthat, a columnist for the *New York Times*, read Rod Dreher's Benedict Option project in this vein. In an op-ed, he described the Benedict Option not as a checklist of practices but as an "invitation to sort of [a] religious ratchet, in which people start from wherever they are and then take one step towards a greater rigor and coherence in the way they marry faith and life".[2] The Benedict Option, here, is simply a catchier name for "try, each day, to be a bit more like Christ" or, more succinctly, "be a Christian."

Narrowing our focus on the Benedict Option's emphasis on offering and receiving hospitality can help us, just as monastic rules do. It gives us concrete ways to build up certain virtues and helps us to find vivid examples to learn from. But it brings with it the temptation to take the part for the whole and to imagine God as smaller than He is: we take one facet of His goodness (be it hospitality, bravery, or anything else) and elevate it above other virtues.

Romanticizing our commitment to the Benedict Option or any other spiritual practice leads to pride and other sins. Although the concept of the BenOp may be new, this kind of attendant temptation is not. More than thirty years ago, Father Alexander Schmemann, an Orthodox priest, expressed in his journal his exasperation with a growing infatuation with monasticism that was taking hold among

---

[2] Ross Douthat, "Christians in the Hands of Donald Trump", *New York Times*, March 15, 2017, https://www.nytimes.com/2017/03/15/opinion /christians-in-the-hands-of-donald-trump.html.

the people he pastored. He found that these enthusiasts were attracted to what he labeled the "vaudeville" of cenobitic life in community. He preferred to advise a person who felt a calling to monastic life to take up unromantic disciplines. His recommendations included the following:

- Get a job, if possible the simplest one, without creativity (for example as a cashier in a bank). While working, pray and seek inner peace; do not get angry; do not think of yourself (rights, fairness, etc.). Accept everyone (coworkers, clients) as someone sent to you; pray for them. After paying for a modest apartment and groceries, give your money to the poor; to individuals rather than foundations.
- Always go to the same church and there try to be a real helper, not by lecturing about spiritual life or icons, not by teaching but with a "dust rag" (cf. St Seraphim of Sarov). Keep at that kind of service and be in church matters totally obedient to the parish priest.
- Do not thrust yourself and your service on anyone; do not be sad that your talents are not being used; be helpful; serve where needed and not where you think you are needed.
- Be always simple, light, joyous. Do not teach. Avoid like the plague any "spiritual" conversations and any religious or churchly idle talk. If you act that way, everything will be to your benefit.[3]

I recognized myself in Schmemann's complaint. Before I began dating my husband, I wanted to give God a chance

---

[3] *The Journals of Father Alexander Schmemann, 1973–1983* (New York: St. Vladimir's Seminary Press, 2000), 284.

to tell me if He were calling me to religious life, and I spent a little time researching different orders. I was most attracted to the Nashville Dominicans and their charism of teaching. But, when I thought a little harder about *what* was drawing me toward them, I realized I was mostly picturing myself as a teacher—a teacher wearing a habit.

I was responding to the sisters' teaching work, not to their gift of their whole lives to God. I was missing the heart of what it means to be a consecrated religious woman. I visited the sisters and was blessed by their hospitality and the opportunity to join in their prayers, but I didn't discern further with their community.

Back out in the world, what I found most helpful in Schmemann's instruction was his warning to "serve where needed and not where you think you are needed." The enemies of Christian community—be they the long work hours that leave no room for the Sabbath, the devaluation of nonerotic love, or the weakening (and shrinking) of families—may shape the way I am needed. But I don't want to get so excited about my own ideas and solutions that I miss the chance to hear God's. I want to develop my readiness to be used by God, to be responsive to His promptings.

It's easiest for me to resist the temptation to go haring off after imagined needs and enemies when I force myself to stay grounded. I turn my eyes away from ideological enemies or societal errors, and I pay attention to the specific needs of one friend or even my own moments of loneliness. If I respond to immediate needs, and not to my theories of need, I have a better chance of serving where I am needed.

When I'm tempted to wait for something "important" to do, I try to stay attentive to all the small needs that God might be offering me the chance to meet. And I try to remember that sometimes He's waiting for me to help by offering my needs to Him or to a friend, letting someone be Christ to me, instead of holding myself aloof. The Benedict Option, as I practice it, is a crutch, not a glamorous charism. Creating community throws me into the paths of others, giving me more chances to learn to love them and to let them love me. I need practice in imitating Christ, so I place myself in spaces where the needs of others will be louder, where I may hear them and respond.

Many of the threats to the Benedict Option are my own temptations and weaknesses, such as pride. There are external threats built into our society, however, that make Christian life harder to practice—and even to imagine.

Loneliness and the Limited Family

A friend of mine complained to me once, "If I don't get married, no one will be able to take care of me when I'm sick." She wasn't being overdramatic: even with friends who care about her, it's frighteningly true. As a matter of law, sick-leave policies give workers time off to care for a child or a spouse or a parent, but not a friend. That's "vacation" time, if you have some you can use.

And even when friends are willing to help, they may be too far flung to do as much as they would like to. When I sprained my ankle while traveling, I was very blessed by the kindness of strangers (including the woman who let me hitchhike with her to look for a cane). When I got home, I was able to rely on my husband as well as my mother and brother, who came to stay with me while my husband was at work. There were so many kinds of help I couldn't imagine asking of my friends. I needed help getting a glass of water, changing an ice pack, and even getting to the bathroom; someone who lived forty minutes away by subway couldn't do much to help with those sudden needs.

Our lives are built not around friends but around family, and a narrow idea of family at that. Families are shrinking, and as children grow up with fewer (or zero) brothers and sisters, it's not just siblings they wind up missing. Andrew Yuengert wrote in an essay for the blog *Front Porch Republic*:

> The fact that the number of parents and grandparents is stable may distract us from the collapse in the number of aunts/uncles and cousins. For example, when average family size falls from four to three, each person loses a sibling, of course, but he or she also loses four aunts and uncles and twelve cousins. The collapse to one child wipes out the siblings, but it also wipes out the aunts/uncles and cousins.[4]

Small families can't produce the kind of joyful scrum of relatives that Louisa May Alcott's Rose discovers in *Eight Cousins*, when she goes to stay with her extended family, all living on what she calls "Aunt Hill". When a family sprawls, there's more room to sneak friends into the fold as well. With four or five aunts already, what's one more "Auntie" who acquires the name by being close friends with one of your parents rather than by blood? If a child has only one aunt, a friend who might want to adopt the appellation is horning in on a more exclusive relationship.

As a little girl, I recognized that one of my mother's college friends was going to be a part of my life and my mother's forever. I dubbed her my "honorary grandmother". Mary was the wrong age for the title, but both of my grandmothers had passed away before I was born,

---

[4] Andrew Yuengert, "The Family Tree, Stripped", *Front Porch Republic*, February 3, 2015, http://www.frontporchrepublic.com/2015/02/family-tree -stripped/.

and, as far as a preschooler like me could tell, Mary did all the things a grandmother should do. She taught me to sew and to embroider, she made my first baby blanket, and every year, just before Christmas, she came to our house to bake cookies with my brother and me. With her example in mind, now that I'm grown up, I've tried to become an honorary aunt to the child of one of my friends by visiting Theodora and her mom, traveling across the country to see their family when work made them move away, and introducing my husband to the family I thought of as part of my family too.

Playwright Sarah Ruhl notes that while *Death of a Salesman* has fourteen characters, many modern family dramas have casts of only four to six characters. She wonders, "Did the rise of birth control and smaller families correspond to the diminishment of cast size, and if so, what then? On stage, a small family becomes a symbol of neurosis, whereas a large family becomes a microcosm of the world." Modern playwrights, she continued, "tend to write about smaller families as though there was no world outside their living room."[5] A Christian can feel just as constricted as a playwright, when families feel too sparse to be the "school of deeper humanity".[6]

More Than Marriage

In the Israeli film *The Wedding Plan*, the Orthodox Jewish protagonist, Michal, is jilted by her fiancé and decides to

[5] Sarah Ruhl, *100 Essays I Don't Have Time to Write: On Umbrellas and Sword Fights, Parades and Dogs, Fire Alarms, Children, and Theater* (New York: Farrar, Straus, and Giroux, 2014), 87.

[6] Vatican Council II, Pastoral Constitution on the Church in the Modern World *Gaudium et spes* (December 7, 1965), no. 52, http://www.vatican.va/archive/hist_councils/ii_vatican_council/documents/vat-ii_cons_19651207_gaudium-et-spes_en.html.

hold her scheduled wedding ceremony, trusting God to provide the groom. At the beginning of the film, she prays with another woman, who asks her what it is that she wants. Michal says she wants to be married, she wants love, but her companion tells her that these are lies and presses her to admit what she's really seeking. Michal bursts into tears and says she wants to be able to invite people into her home for Shabbat dinner, instead of always being a guest in someone else's home. Wants spill out of her, many of them just as small and humble: she wants a home, for which marriage seems to be a prerequisite.

In Michal's culture and in ours, marriage is too often treated as a be-all and end-all. Even as no-fault divorce and other cultural changes diminish the meaning of marriage, the institution is expected to mean more and more. If marriage is treated as what makes us whole, young men and women may find themselves spinning their wheels, waiting for their vows before making a gift of themselves to another, at a loss for how they might offer what Christ calls the greatest form of love, to lay down their lives for their friends (see Jn 15:13). Even after marriage, it is easy to miss opportunities to offer love to friends and to receive love from them, if a couple lacks practice with self-giving as an expression of nonerotic love.

As celibate gay Christians, Eve Tushnet and Wesley Hill are canaries in the coal mine. They know they can't live life before marriage as a forgettable prologue to the rest of their lives. With marriage out of the picture, they've thought deeply about how our society sidelines friendship and consigns both single and married people to a loneliness that would have been unimaginable in previous cultures of Boston marriages, extended families, and lively street blocks.

Tushnet saw in a Pixar short, *Lava*, a portrait of the narrow way in which we imagine love. The film follows a lonely volcano, warbling his yearning for someone to "love-a". In despair, he sinks into the ocean, until a new volcano (with implausibly delicate, feminine features) erupts beside him and they conclude with a duet. Tushnet saw the film as speaking to a common fear, that unless we are paired off, we will be abandoned. She wrote, "We are terrified of being alone with nobody to help us. And the only, or at least the ideal and normative, escape from loneliness is romantic love. There are no children in this cartoon and no community. The gulls have no chicks, and the fish have no school."[7]

In a follow-up essay about the Pixar short, Tushnet argued that the story told there, like many modern stories, is about love that saves us from loneliness, not love that requires discipline or sacrifice. It is the "You complete me" model of romantic love, in which the lovers come to rest in their marriage; their coming together is the end of their story. Tushnet wrote:

> We've moved from viewing marriage as an institution that restrains heterosexual eros (both premarital and marital sexuality) and helps it to be somewhat more fruitful and less destructive than it would be otherwise, to viewing marriage as the solution to the problem of aloneness, the solution to personal isolation and social fragmentation. Marriage as constraint has become marriage as comfort, perhaps marriage as self-expression, even marriage as release. Marriage is the reward for achieving responsible love, rather than the institution that helps us, slowly, make our love responsible.[8]

[7] Eve Tushnet, "Being Single Shouldn't Mean Being Alone", *Washington Post*, February 10, 2016, https://www.washingtonpost.com/news/in-theory/wp/2016/02/10/being-single-shouldnt-mean-being-alone/?utm_term=.56edf2a2b55b.

[8] Eve Tushnet, "'Lava' in the Western World: Justice Kennedy and Pixar", *Patheos*, June 27, 2015, http://www.patheos.com/blogs/evetushnet/2015/06/lava-in-the-western-world-justice-kennedy-and-pixar.html.

That notion of marriage is alien to Christians, who, even when in love, still have the restless heart that harried Saint Augustine. Our hearts are restless until they rest in God. Husband and wife can help each other traverse the exodus of our earthly life, but they cannot be the end of the journey. Fifty years before Tushnet and Pixar, Robert Farrar Capon, an Episcopal priest, in his compendium of marriage advice, warned prospective couples to avoid this sort of error. He wrote:

> People in love usually act as if the whole process meant that they were supposed to find their fulfillment in each other—as if they were, respectively, each other's final goal. "You're the only girl in the world for me." "We were meant for each other." That, of course, is nonsense if you believe Dante. They were not meant for each other; they were meant to communicate the glory to each other. They are not gods, but ministers. Beatrice is precisely a priestly figure. She is not my destiny, but the agent, the delightful sacrament, of it. If I treat her as an end, delight is about all I can bargain for, and not even that for long. If I take her as a sacrament, I receive, along with the delight, the joy that lies behind her.[9]

Capon's advice here is as applicable to friends as to married couples. Any person we love, and even those we barely know and those we dislike, may serve as "ministers of the glory" to us. When we are sent out of Mass, carrying Christ within us in the Eucharist, when we spend time in silent prayer, asking God to fill us with His Spirit, we are sent forth to communicate that glory and grace to others. Because we are acting for God and He is acting through

[9] Robert Farrar Capon, *Bed and Board: Plain Talk about Marriage* (New York: Pocket Books, 1970), 66.

us, we are capable of far more than we could do if we were relying only on our own strength.

Countercultural Friendship

Wesley Hill suggests that the best way to start deepening friendships is to "ask ourselves whom we're already bound to and how we might strengthen *those* bonds".[10] That might mean repairing a broken relationship, but Hill expects that it will usually be a matter of "choos[ing] to invite our friends to become more regular fixtures of our lives". He suggests making standing commitments: "walking the dogs together on Tuesday mornings or walking to the corner coffee shop after dropping the kids off at preschool on Thursdays".[11] His suggestions aren't extravagant; they're a way to weave friends into the quotidian rhythms of our lives. These plans are a commitment to see friends *by default*, making fellowship the path of least resistance.

In deeper, stronger friendships, Hill can imagine more effusive habits of love. He befriends a couple when he begins seeing them at a larger weekly gathering, and soon he and the pair plan to have dinner together once a week. The three friends make plans to find a place to live that they can all share, one that would include Hill while still allowing privacy and intimacy for the married couple. Ultimately, his friends turn down a tempting job opportunity to avoid moving away from their beloved friend. He becomes their daughter's godfather.

---

[10] Wesley Hill, *Spiritual Friendship: Finding Love in the Church as a Celibate Gay Christian* (Grand Rapids: Brazos, 2015), 108.
[11] Ibid.

Hill's housemates aren't the first couple to commit to a deeper friendship with him, one that becomes a kind of adoption into their family. When he was a graduate student in England, he was welcomed by another student and his wife. The three shared dinner several times a week. Hill describes their routine:

> Sometimes I helped Megan cook dinner. I would sit beside high chairs smeared with mashed green beans.... Usually I would do the dishes afterward as the kids were bathed and put to bed, and the three of us, along with other friends sometimes, would try to unwind with a bottle of wine in the living room and episodes of *Friday Night Lights*. I wasn't so much a guest as I was an uncle, an expected face in their normal, unprettified lives—a relational status that was eventually sealed when I stood as a godparent for their second child's baptism.[12]

In both of these friendships, the love that Hill and his friends shared was sealed by the arrival of a child. Becoming a godparent to these families' children created a permanent bond between him and his friends, one that lasted past the end of his graduate program and his return to the States, and one that will endure even if he and his current housemates find that they need to split up. It is a serious gap in our culture and our language that there isn't a word to describe what Hill is to these families, except for the title the children give him through their baptism. That makes it harder to imagine, long for, and pursue these kinds of love.

Thin friendships that never deepen in the way that Hill's do leave single people and married people isolated, emotionally and physically. Hill may end the evening

[12] Wesley Hill, "Jigs for Marriage and Celibacy", *Comment*, November 24, 2016, https://www.cardus.ca/comment/article/4987/jigs-for-marriage-and -celibacy/.

sharing a couch with his close friends, but affectionate, platonic touch has evaporated from the lives of many modern Americans. Even at church, the passing of the peace has atrophied from a kiss to a handshake to a stilted wave. Tushnet argues in favor of returning to the kiss, as a countercultural witness to a culture that has let sexuality squeeze out affectionate friendship. In an essay, she writes:

> In many Western countries we've sexualized all physical intimacy.... Some translations of the Bible have John reclining "next to Jesus" rather than against Jesus' breast. We've made physical touch the exclusive property of sexual relationships, and so, unsurprisingly, we starve for it. We all need to be touched, to know that our bodies are viewed with love and welcome.[13]

Hill echoes Tushnet's call to take up arms (and all the rest of the body) against recasting the body as purely sexual. He recounts the outburst of one of his professors, who bristles at the idea that Christians should simply endure physical lonelines: "It's no use trying to be more spiritual than God, you know! God is the one who created humans to want and need relationships, to crave human companionship.... God wants people to experience his love through their experience of human community, specifically, the church. God created us physical-spiritual beings with deep longings for intimacy with other physical-spiritual beings. We're not meant to replace these longings with anything. We're meant to sanctify them."[14]

---

[13] Eve Tushnet, "The Kiss of Peace: Liturgy to Free Us from Our Isolation", *Level Ground*, November 5, 2014, https://www.onlevelground.org/blog archives/dialogue/the-kiss-of-peace-liturgy-to-free-us-from-our-isolation.

[14] Wesley Hill, *Washed and Waiting: Reflections on Christian Faithfulness and Homosexuality* (Grand Rapids: Zondervan, 2016), 130.

Trying to do without the support of others, whether expressed through physical affection or in shared worship, is a kind of starvation. In Paul's First Letter to the Corinthians, he reminds us that the Church is composed of many members, all dependent on God but dependent on Him *through* each other. Each part cannot serve in isolation, he writes: "If the whole body were an eye, where would be the hearing? If the whole body were an ear, where would be the sense of smell?" (12:17). We suffer when we separate ourselves through pride and when we find ourselves separated, through circumstances, from the other parts of the one body of the Church.

Weak Witness of Others

For some Christians, that isolation begins in the home. People who have grown up weakly Catholic (or, rather, as merely weekly Catholics) might not know what practicing their faith could mean, beyond going to church once a week. Other young adults might feel that all of their traditions of prayer are embedded in their family's home and that they don't know how to keep that flame alive on their own, how to step into the role their parents had, as the leaders of worship.

My husband is also a convert to Catholicism (his family entered the Church en masse), but during his childhood, his family were fiercely faithful Anglo-Catholics, and his parents brought him up in a lively, prayer-filled home. On Saturday nights, his family prayed together in anticipation of the Lord's Day on Sunday. Led by his parents, he and his family lit a candle, shared blessed bread and wine, and gave thanks to God.

This would have been a hard tradition for him to keep up, on his own, in college. It's hard to smuggle wine into a dining hall, and the candle would be even more likely to prompt censure (open flames being seen as more volatile than alcohol). After college, the prayer only gets harder to keep up: how can you say a prayer with call and response if there's no one there to respond to, no one in your home with whom to break bread?

For people who grow up with thick prayer practices, as my husband did, even when these prayers no longer fit into our changing lives, they bring a gift: we miss them. Sensing a hollowness or a gap in the rhythms of our day can prompt us to fill it. If the old practice doesn't fit the new shape of our lives (and it doesn't make sense to reshape our lives to make it work again), we try to find something else to add, to help us return to God.

As a convert, I try to catch the hunger for prayer habits from my husband and from other passionate Christian friends, both those who were raised in the faith and those who entered the Church as adults, like me. I'm lucky to have a pen pal who is a nun, a friend I met after my conversion, who joined the Dominican Sisters of Hawthorne. She offers hospice care to the dying poor, she prays with her fellow sisters throughout the day, and, in her little spare time, she writes to me. In our letters to each other, we tend to write only of ourselves, of God, and of the relationship between the three of us. Our letters aren't frequent enough to be diverted by the daily news; with her as my audience, I write about what persists. And I love to receive her letters, because the ferocity of her love and her intimacy with Christ shine out of every page.

In a milder way, I'm also spiritually fed by a group of friends who comprise "Weird Christian Twitter", only some of whom I've met in person. When I exchange thoughts or share links with them, I get the chance to talk about our faith in a way that hasn't been shaped by the world—well, not shaped *as much*; it's hard to shake off worldliness completely.

But, while the mainstream news stories on religion that I read are nearly always about what is most controversial about our faith—the latest political clash over church-state boundaries; the newest misinterpretations of another informal, off-the-cuff remark from Pope Francis; the religious practices that most rankle secular culture—the things my friends share are much more likely to be prompted by joy. One friend shared a striking painting of Mary and Elizabeth in the Visitation; another snapped a photo of a moving passage in a book by the Church Fathers that he was reading; another told a funny story about her preschool-age daughter getting off her scooter to kiss the cross in front of a Methodist church (surprising some nearby members).

Our families and our friends can be our links to the small-*c* catholicity of our universal Church. They steady us in our prayer practices and keep turning us back to Christ, the heart of our faith. But for anyone whose family is only casually Catholic, whose friends can't join him in communion, whose parish's homilies cover current events without ever drawing on the richness of our two-thousand-year history, living as a Catholic means living as a missionary, without the help that many missionaries have as part of a larger, if far away, institution. As Dreher says in *The Benedict Option*, "We cannot give the world what we do not have."[15] We cannot call others to conversion if we don't know Him to whom we are consecrated.

Nibbled-Away Time

I've been lucky to work for employers who respect a clear distinction between being on and off the clock. In my

---

[15] Rod Dreher, *The Benedict Option: A Strategy for Christians in a Post-Christian Nation* (New York: Sentinel, 2017), 19.

first job after college, I was pleased to discover that my position was classified as "nonexempt", meaning that I wasn't exempt from rules requiring overtime pay. As my boss explained it to me, I should never check my work e-mail outside of work, because I could put the company on the hook for paying me time and a half for those ten minutes spent replying. So I was surprised to find my housemate, Alexander, who worked in a similar position and under the same rules, asking me if I had seen an e-mail from our boss that evening. He had set up push notifications on his phone, so that he was always instantaneously alerted to messages. I scolded him, telling him that he wasn't just shortchanging himself, but he was also breaking the rules, and he ought to turn the notifications off.

Most of my friends weren't as lucky as Alexander and I were. Although a number of them might have been working under the same classification as I was, their bosses didn't have the talk with them that mine had with me. For some friends in journalism, working some nights and weekends was a given: their bosses wanted to have someone on call, in case major news broke. For others, there was no need for round-the-clock coverage, but their bosses assigned more work than could be done during business hours and left it to their staff to figure out how to get it done. Other friends had work with variable hours (scheduled by their bosses, not by them) or hours that inverted their work-free time (a friend who became a cook began referring to the rest of us as "daywalkers").

That made it hard to expect that we could gather in the evenings or on weekends. Even if my friends didn't have social commitments, they weren't always sure if they had work-related obligations. It didn't get better when I lived in Berkeley, California, for a year, and many of my friends were programmers who didn't have any specific work hours at all. The ones who founded startups had given their lives to their companies, and the ones who were smaller cogs in bigger companies had plenty of inducements—free dinners, on-site laundry, and so forth—to keep them at their offices and working.

At one point, my supervisor asked me, intending to be generous, if there was anything that I'd like our tiny company to change for my benefit. Was there a food the company should stock, a way to reconfigure my desk, anything at all that would make the office more attractive to me, so I might want to stay later? I replied, as politely as I could, that I didn't want my job to be in the business of coaxing me to stay later. I was doing work that interested me, for a project I thought was important, but it was never going to be the axis around which my life turned.

My friends and I felt pinched by the voraciousness of our work for more of our selves, but we still were relatively lucky; nearly all of us held comfortably paid white-collar jobs. We didn't have to contend with balancing work, life, and a second round of work at an extra job, taken to make ends meet. Few of us came home bone-tired from physical labor, suffering from exhaustion or chronic pain that cast a pall over whatever time our jobs left us.

Across industries, employers may expect their workers to be oblates—a word derived from "offering" and historically used to describe people offered to the Church as monks and nuns. But whereas a life given over to prayer and adoration reshapes our soul, helping us to pattern ourselves after Christ, a life given to spreadsheets and Powerpoints—even ones dedicated to a good cause—can be deadening to the soul. We are created to be more than what any job can ask of us; if we grow only to fit the needs of our work, we will be stunted.

The Absence of Stability

In my first five years after college, I held six jobs and lived in two cities (or, rather, three cities if you count a two-month stint at my parents' home while I was between jobs). Saying that I lived in two cities is a little oversimplified, though. In Washington, D.C., I lived in five residences, never with the same set of housemates. In California, I had so much trouble finding a room in Berkeley's tight housing market that I spent my first four months couch surfing or cadging week-long sublets before finally coming to rest in a group house I hated (ten people, few of whom I knew, none of whom seemed to wash dishes).

For most of that time, I operated under the assumption that everything around me was temporary. My jobs frequently had end dates (a spring internship, a ten-month fellowship, a six-month trial period). When I took each of these jobs, I knew that I would soon need to move on and that it would be difficult to find my next job in the same city. I could be at rest for only the first two or three months of these jobs, and then it was time to start searching again.

I was never more miserable than when I lived my life on an ad hoc, temporary basis. I moved my posters to a new apartment but never put them up, figuring I would simply need to take them down again. I didn't join a gym, because I wouldn't be able to commit to a year-long contract. I couldn't make commitments to parish groups, knowing I would be leaving before the lecture series was over.

The silliest thing I denied myself because of my lack of stability was a sourdough starter. I had enjoyed keeping and feeding and cooking with a starter, but I threw it out when I made my cross-country move and didn't feel as if

I were allowed to have a new one. It felt foolish to keep feeding a starter if I might soon move again and would either have to find a way to transport the bubbly mess or else scrape it into the garbage again. So I gave up making sourdough bread and pizza dough. I gave up surprising my housemates with sourdough pancakes when I needed to find *something* to do with the excess. I gave up the fun of tending to such a weird sort of living thing.

I felt too guilty about the possibility that my unsettled life would make me wrong a sourdough starter— something lower than a plant. Starter is just a mix of yeast, water, and partially digested flour. If I felt that I had to be that conservative about making commitments to a microorganism, what was I too chary to commit to offering or receiving from other people?

People do require even more of me than sourdough starters, but I wronged my potential friends and myself when I kept waiting for moments of prolonged peace to take on commitments to others. There were some kinds of promises I couldn't make: it would have been wrong to sign a long-term lease with a friend if I expected to leave the city soon. My precarious life required me to make real forfeitures. But it was foolish to hold myself back from knitting myself to my friends, even if those bonds would be stretched, frayed, or even torn apart by the moves either of us might make.

I take heart from the profligacy of the saints. There's a kind of spendthrift nature in loving others in a way you don't know if you can sustain. Even if your love will be tested or permanently disrupted by a move, by unpredictable hours, or by a lack of societal support from friends and family who don't know how to shore up nonromantic love, it is still worth sharing. "The morrow shall take thought for the things of itself" (Mt 6:34, KJV), but today, it's simply my job to love others as Christ does, for however long He grants me to love and to be loved by them. It's for God to sort out how that love will blossom and be transfigured.

When I was an atheist, I felt more pressure to bring projects or relationships to a successful completion. If I had a disagreement with someone and neither of us changed his mind, if I enjoyed seeing someone but never made a deeper connection, I felt I had left something undone. As an atheist, I didn't believe there was anyone out there supporting my efforts; what I left unfinished was unfinished forever.

As a Catholic, I feel more like a participant in a relay race. I run the leg of love that is before me this day or even this minute, and I trust God to make something of it. When I think of my conversion, I can see that I was helped along the way by many small conversations and friendships that, in the moment, seemed to be bearing no fruit. But, in the fullness of time, sometimes a "wasted" conversation prepared me to be receptive to the person whose arguments struck home for me. The seeds these friends (and even passing acquaintances) offered me may have fallen on stony ground, but their attention softened the hard ground and made it ready to receive the gifts others offered me.

When we stare down the enemies of the Benedict Option, we must keep in mind that we have been promised that we are not fighting a losing war. Despite attacks on our stability, on our time, on our capacity to love, we have every reason to be fearless and profligate with the gifts God has given us. "I know the plans I have for you", God says in Jeremiah, "plans to prosper you and not to harm you" (Jer 29:11, NIV). If we look at God's love for His Son, we know that those prosperous plans require us to endure pain. We must conform ourselves to the Cross and be transfigured by God. Although external enemies may surround us "like bees" (Ps 118:12), in the end, only our choice to shrink away from God's love and to refuse to share it with others can endanger our souls.

3

The Beginning of My Benedict Option

Like very few good things, our BenOp project started as a fight on Twitter. In April 2015, a bunch of my friends (along with some strangers) were having an argument about the Benedict Option, 140 characters at a time. Rod Dreher's book hadn't come out yet, so the discussion was rooted in whatever he had posted on his blog to date—plus any rebuttals or responses written elsewhere that anyone chose to link into the sprawling subthreads.

I liked the Benedict Option as I understood it, but I really didn't want to try to describe what I imagined a thick, vibrant Christian community could be by replying in tweets. Twitter is a great way to see articles or photos my friends share or to hear pithy updates on their day, but it's a poorly suited forum for a substantive discussion.

That was my general objection to having complicated conversations on Twitter, but there was a further problem with this particular discussion. I kept noticing that a number of my friends objected to the BenOp as "fleeing to the hills" or "turning our backs on society". But they seemed to be debating a nonexistent group. There were plenty of people in the reply chains who said that they were pro-BenOp, but when they praised it, they weren't talking about the vision that the anti-retreat group objected to. (This pattern has persisted even since the publication of Dreher's book.)

We kept muddling two conversations: (1) What *is* the Benedict Option? and (2) Is the Benedict Option (whatever it is) a good idea? It's quicker (which counts for a lot on Twitter) to answer both questions together by identifying a project or a vision of the BenOp that you dislike as the heart of the idea and then rejecting it. It's much harder to articulate *any* of the possible positive visions of the movement in compressed tweets. I wanted to make space to talk about whatever attracted people to the Benedict Option, instead of beginning with objections and critiques. In nearly all fights, I think it helps to start by hearing out the side that *wants* something, since it's their goal that others are trying to understand and either quash or pursue. When it came to the BenOp, I wanted to begin by hearing about what people actually wanted to do, not what they planned never to do, because the anti-BenOppers could (and would) simply go on not doing the things they objected to.

So, I invited the Internet into my home. It had worked at least once before, when I got my friends to agree to suspend a nasty fight about politics that they were having on my Facebook wall, with the promise that they could resume the argument in person, in my living room, as a debate moderated by Robert's Rules of Order. For the BenOp event, I didn't plan anything quite so structured. We were all Christians and on the same side: wanting to do a better job living out our vocation to be saints, and supporting each other in that calling. We were arguing about means, not ends. Plus, we could start and end the night in prayer, relying on God to smooth our way.

I e-mailed about sixty people, including everyone in the original Twitter fight who lived in or near my home city of Washington, D.C., and any Catholic or Eastern Orthodox friends who I was confident would be game for a "doing a better job of being Christian" discussion, whether or not they had heard of the Benedict Option. I polled them all on their schedules, and about thirty people committed to come over for an in-person discussion. I asked people for suggested essays to read beforehand and shared a curated list,[1] but there was no official homework. My guests needed only to come with both a desire to be more like Christ and a bit of confusion about how to do so.

Although the two questions animating our Twitter conversation had been "What *is* the Benedict Option?" and "Is the BenOp a good idea?", I took a different approach to structuring the event I hosted. I split our discussion into two parts. We started the night on the roof of my building. We prayed, we ate pasta, and then I opened the floor to *any* kind of discussion of the Benedict Option. In the final thirty to forty-five minutes of the event, I made a deliberate shift. We trooped downstairs to my apartment, ate chocolate bourbon cake, and had a more restricted conversation. During the first phase, any BenOp-related thought was kosher, but in the latter phase, I limited the discussion to ideas that attendees were considering carrying out within the next three months.

A BenOp Boring Enough to Be Unstoppable

The anything-goes roof conversation got to be broad and wild. People talked about what kind of homeschooling

[1] Peter Blair, "Benedict Option Reading Suggestions (Updated)", *Fare Forward*, May 21, 2015, http://farefwd.com/2015/05/benedict-option-reading -suggestions/.

collective they might want to set up (years from now), batted around the idea of cohousing (one day, when more of us could think about mortgages), mentioned political fears, and so on. A lot of the roof discussion centered on the tension of being the salt of the earth while not being the salt that loses its saltiness (see Mt 5:13).

And then, in the middle of a discussion about counter-cultural witness and whether Christians should always stick out a bit, never fully assimilated into any kingdom of this world, one of the attendees sighed and said, "Of course, whatever we do, the Leviathan State will eventually turn its eye on us and crush us."

I could grant that that was true of the weirdest (and even some of the less weird) BenOp ideas my friends had floated. One of the most extreme, an underground nurse service in a future America that had crushed all conscience laws, definitely sounded illegal—and definitely of interest to the state. Having two families or a group of unmarried friends buy a house together wasn't anywhere near as wild, but, in many neighborhoods, it was often just as illegal. In New York City, and in many other places across the country, zoning laws prohibit more than three unrelated adults from living together (though the law is not always enforced).[2]

There might be times when we should consider breaking these or other laws and taking the consequences that come with civil disobedience. But I was darned sure that there were plenty of ways for us to care for each other, pray for each other, and become more like Christ that were way too boring for the state to care about. Once we went downstairs and started talking about specific projects

[2] Cara Buckley, "In New York, Breaking a Law on Roommates", *New York Times*, March 28, 2010, http://www.nytimes.com/2010/03/29/nyregion /29roommates.html.

we could take on in the next few months, the brainstorming bore me out.

As part of our discussion, I asked my friends just to name things they wanted out of the Benedict Option. Upstairs, we talked more about institutions or traditions, but downstairs, I wanted to hear what people needed *now*. It was easy for worries about what we would do when we had children to swamp any more petty-feeling needs we had right then, but I wanted to know how to serve my friends as they were. Asking for wants, I wasn't promising to find a way to solve everyone's problems, or that *anyone* in the room was going to step up, or even that the problems were solvable. I was just aiming for a census of wants. I hoped that, for some of these wants (including mine), someone else in the circle would turn out to be able to help, but I didn't have more of a plan than just letting these wishes become public.

As people named the things that they wished for— things that they didn't know how to ask for or whom to ask for them—I was struck by how small most of the desires were. My friends wanted such things as "someone to go to Adoration with me" or "someone to sing hymns with" or "someone who will help me learn how to take care of children". Some people wanted to socialize without having to go to noisy and expensive bars and restaurants. The parents in attendance (including two very expectant mothers) hoped for more social events that could work for people who had early bedtimes.

There were harder-to-fulfill desires, too, such as "an Eastern Orthodox parish in D.C. that can be reached without a car". But most of my friends wanted things that were small: desires that didn't require land to be bought or massive projects to be coordinated—wants so small that it felt a little silly to have to ask for them.

50

The BenOp of the Beguines

For all the discussion of the BenOp as "thick" community, it felt as if my friends and I were asking simply for community, even a relatively thin one. So many of their wants were things that didn't require a best friend or a love deeper than storgé (the fondness that comes from seeing someone repeatedly).

We wanted opportunities to love that didn't require us to have our lives already sorted out or to know what job we would hold next or what city we would live in a few years from now. (I once startled a job interviewer who asked me what my five-year plan for myself was, when I answered, "Oh, I've learned to stop making those!") If we didn't have the wherewithal to found towns, schools, or other deeply rooted institutions, what kind of gifts could we offer? Several people brought up one historical BenOp project we all felt a little envious of, a model that seemed almost within our reach: beguinages.

Beguinages lay somewhere between monasteries and lay life. They were the homes of women in Europe called beguines, and they existed on and off from the thirteenth to the sixteenth century. The beguines who came together in a beguinage committed to shared prayer and communal life, without making a permanent plan or vow. When they could, they found ways to share their homes, too. Laura Swan, a historian of monasticism, offers an introduction to life in these communities in *The Wisdom of the Beguines*:

> Their convents usually were comprised of anywhere from three to twenty-four women. Many beguines preferred to live in such smaller groups, which made it easier to "move on" when new ministry or preaching opportunities emerged. Elements of daily life in such convents were

similar to life in court beguinages: gathering for prayer and celebration of mass (but at the local parish church rather than their own chapel or church), tending to business enterprises to support themselves and their ministries, and doing household tasks. Court beguinages required more of an individual beguine's time to support basic operations of the community, which somewhat limited her available time for—and choice of—ministry. Court beguinages were usually also supporting large numbers of indigent beguines, often known as *paupercule begine*, which required a commitment of the entire women's community....

Friends invited friends to join their beguine community. Aunts invited nieces. Cousins invited cousins. Rarely were total strangers invited to join—until they were known and had become friends with the beguines. In established beguine communities, a room might become available and an invitation would be extended.... A woman would be invited to live with the community on a trial basis—usually for one year—and then there would be a welcoming ceremony within the house. If she fit in and was content with the life there, she continued to live on a trial basis with the community for another year or so. After these initial two years, the woman—after her request to become a beguine had been accepted by the house members or the council of elders—would be invited to a clothing ceremony, accepting the attire of a beguine.[3]

While living in a beguinage, beguines might support themselves through work. They might leave to get married, or they might remain a part of the community for most of their lives. Some of the best-known beguines were mystics, but most beguines led relatively ordinary lives,

---

[3] Laura Swan, *The Wisdom of the Beguines: The Forgotten Story of a Medieval Women's Movement* (New York: BlueBridge, 2014), 56–57.

except insofar as they were infused with shared service to God.

This flexible model of shared worship and support, with people cycling in and out, as their lives permitted, was closer to what many of us wished the BenOp could be for us, right then. We weren't ready to commit to a cohousing model where we bought neighboring homes, but we could try to find apartments in a single building or in a block and have a beguinage hidden inside an otherwise ordinary building.

Offering Anything, Even the Wrong Things

The idea of a modern-day beguinage kept (and keeps) enchanting me and my friends, but we're still scattered across the city (at best) and the country (at worst). Although some individuals managed to become housemates, for most of us, our Benedict Option projects have been much smaller. We haven't been able to establish any long-term shared spaces, but we create ephemeral ones each time one of us opens his house for a dinner, a prayer session, or a discussion. We offer what we can, hoping to get into the habit of hospitality, and asking God to prompt us to offer more—to trust in Him whenever a chance opens up.

One of the barriers to our hoped-for beguinages was the puzzle of lease terms. I had missed opportunities to live with friends when we wound up on leases that ended many months apart. It was hard to sync up to move in together. It was also harder than I expected to find a neighborhood that many of us could easily move into. Different metro lines sprawled across the city, all questionably reliable, so, unless I organized a group house based on Red Line ridership, how could I reasonably ask friends to add a half hour or an hour to their commute by starting on the wrong line? The goal was to have a home we all wanted to spend time in, and the wrong liners would be spending that time in metro tunnels instead. I had found a place for myself downtown, at the intersection of all the lines, to make it easy for friends to visit, but that sought-after location would price out many of my friends who were students, burdened by college debt, or working in low-paying industries. (I afforded my place by taking a windowless den for my bedroom and paying a lower rate than my housemates.)

What we were going to build, within the next three months, might be inspired by the beguinages, but it wasn't going to live up to them. We were scrappier, trying to scrabble for any piece of community we could build together. We might suspect that, logistically, we were the seeds sown on rocky ground, but, for the present, we were just going to try to love each other and rely on God to crack the earth and show us how to root ourselves.

And I found additional encouragement from another source: Rabbi Elie Kaunfer's *Empowered Judaism: What Independent Minyanim Can Teach Us about Building Vibrant Jewish Communities*. Kaunfer had a similar project: bringing together coreligionists to pray together. But the advice I found most helpful in his book wasn't about how to strengthen your prayer group but how to let it go. Kaunfer offered this to organizers whose minyanim (prayer groups) "failed" and stopped meeting: "There is no shame in the dissolution of a minyan.... When people are focused on the purpose of the minyan, rather than the continuation of the minyan as an institution, then that minyan has a better chance of furthering its underlying goals."[4]

[4] Elie Kaunfer, *Empowered Judaism: What Independent Minyanim Can Teach Us about Building Vibrant Jewish Communities* (Woodstock: Jewish Lights, 2010), Kindle edition, location 2579.

I made a conscious effort not to try too hard to make our first project a permanent one. Our starting soil was thin; our initial roots might be shallow. If some events were wholly dependent on my personal enthusiasm or the resources I had, so be it. I focused on simply offering what I could, not worrying too much about making it sustainable.

After our initial BenOp discussion and dinner, I wanted to keep making space for us to eat with each other and to share needs and ideas. So, I started hosting a dinner on the first Friday of every month, for any Christians in D.C. who were interested in the Benedict Option. The dinners didn't have an agenda, as our first discussion did. I just wanted to offer a space for us to share, so that if we wanted to ask things of each other, we would already have the habit of being available to each other. When I moved away from D.C. to get married the dinners stopped; no one had a centrally located and big enough room for hosting or time enough on Fridays for cooking.

Before I moved, I wondered whether I should try to recruit someone to take over the dinners or try to create committees or other structures to share the responsibility. Ultimately, I did neither, and I didn't feel guilty about it. My departure made a difference to the group, and that was all right with me. I didn't want to limit myself to taking on only what I knew my friends and I could sustain. I had belonged to groups that died by committee as people tried to plan out every detail of how we *would* work before we did anything. And there were times I was happy to have things peter out. There's a difference between burning out and overextending yourself experimentally. When you burn out, you walk away exhausted and reluctant to try again, but when you've made an experiment and tried something that may not work, you can continue it or walk away to try your next (possibly) good idea.

The events we couldn't sustain might be the events we no longer needed. If no one had time on Fridays to cook, Friday dinners might not be a good match for the needs and the strengths of our group anymore. If I didn't leave my friends with a specific program of events, I hoped I left them with a readiness to hold whatever event seemed to make the most sense and brought the greatest consolation. At the very beginning of our BenOp push, I believed, and still believe, that if all we did was share a few nights of food and prayer, and then we stopped, that would be enough. No act of love is wasted.

Our Stations of the Cross

Besides, something happened at the first BenOp event that left me confident my friends' generosity would sustain our group, even if we changed shape repeatedly as our circumstances changed. After I asked the attendees at our discussion what they wished for, I asked them what they had to give. My friends mentioned some of the sorts of resources I had expected to elicit: access to a car, a house that was good for events, and so forth. And as it turned out, among everyone, we had both a guitar and a fiddle available, if needed.

People mentioned less-material sorts of resources that they could offer, such as a flexible schedule, which would let them help out at odd hours or make them available to be adult company for stay-at-home parents. Trying to broaden the discussion, I pointed out that one of the pregnant women in the room had the ability to offer several resources we sorely needed. First, and most obviously, she would soon have a baby, and one of our most echoed wishes was to spend time around babies and children, learning to care for them or just enjoying playing with them. But she was also helping our group by being a founding member who had limits on what kinds of events she and her husband could attend.

Having people with constraints was a *resource* for our BenOp group. If we started our project with even one parent whose children's bedtimes required her to head home early, it meant we couldn't make all of our events late-night parties. To serve her, we would need to hold a broader range of events, and, when the next parent befriended one of us, we would already have events he could attend. A newbie wouldn't feel as if he were asking us to create new things just for him.

I sat back, confident that I, the out-of-the-box thinker, had reframed the idea of "resources" for everyone else. And then one of my friends spoke up, offering something that I would never have thought of as a gift. "I've had pretty serious problems with depression," she said. "I guess that means that I can be here for anyone else who's struggling with that, who needs to talk to someone who knows what it's like."

"I'm in recovery for an eating disorder," another person said.

"I'm an alcoholic."

One after another, a half dozen people in the room named some of the worst things that had happened to them and offered them freely as a gift to the rest of us. In some cases, I had already known the cross a friend was carrying, but there were several weights I learned about for the first time that night. To build a BenOp project, my friends moved on from offering conventional strengths and put forward their suffering as their contribution. Because they knew a particular wound, they were ready to minister to someone else enduring it.

I had been managing the meeting, calling on people, taking notes, gently redirecting us when we went off on tangents, but, when my friends offered their crosses, I became too choked up to chair the meeting for a little while. If they could be so generous with some of the hardest parts of their lives, how much could we all give to each other, if we found the courage to ask for what we needed? I thanked God for the gift of these friends and prayed that He would show us how to offer ourselves for each other.

4

The Little Way of Hospitality

In reading essays online about the Benedict Option and about people's biggest hopes for a thick Christian community, many ideas caught my imagination. I could imagine sending children (someday) to a classical Christian school, which would teach Latin, rhetoric, art, and so forth, all with an eye to forming students to see these disciplines through the lens of the Gospels and with the aim of being like Christ. I could imagine (once my husband and I had any idea what city we would live in for more than a year) signing a mortgage as part of a cohousing community, planning to share floors of a townhouse with other Christian families, sharing meals once a week, and having everyone in the house come together daily for Morning Prayer.

The trouble was, all of these big projects required more than my own enthusiasm. They required the substantial commitment of others. Even if a group of us were all ready to pitch in, these projects would require several years to plan and get off the ground. I could picture some people I knew getting started on them (such as my in-laws, already living on a block with neighbors they prayed with as well as for), but my husband and I felt stuck. We didn't have firm enough plans about the future to be able to make this kind of extrafamilial commitment.

I didn't want to wait until we were in our thirties to give and receive love in Christian community, so, in the meantime, I resolved to follow G.K. Chesterton's advice: "If a thing is worth doing, it is worth doing badly."[1] Some of the most exciting BenOp institutions would be beyond me for a while, but nothing could stop me from seizing any small opportunity to love God with my friends. Chesterton's assertion in *What's Wrong with the World* isn't meant as an excuse for slapdash efforts, but as a rallying cry for anyone doing the kind of work that shapes the doer's character.

Parents, friends, and others outsource the work of love to specialists at their peril. Although the experts may appear to produce better results than we amateurs do, there is one important result that delegation will always fail to produce: a change in our own hearts, a strengthening of our own love through service. Chesterton picks up this theme again in *Orthodoxy* when he says that the things we must do ourselves, even if that means doing them badly, are "a thing analogous to writing one's own love-letters or blowing one's own nose".[2]

Trying to worship God with my friends is, I think, a little more analogous to writing my own love letters than to blowing my own nose (even if it is sometimes as messy and confused as the latter). When I try to gather in Christ's name with the people I care about, I am writing love letters to God and to my friends—loving God through worship and loving my friends by sharing the most important part of my life with them.

Love is most fully expressed not through a single grand gesture but through a series of small intimacies. So, when

---

[1] G.K. Chesterton, *What's Wrong with the World*, Gutenberg.org e-edition, chap. 14, https://www.gutenberg.org/files/1717/1717-h/1717-h.htm.

[2] G.K. Chesterton, *Orthodoxy* (New York: Barnes and Noble, 2007), 38.

I tried to figure out what kind of love letters I would be writing by opening my house for BenOp community, I nixed anything that seemed too Pinterest-complex. I wanted to build up everyday, affectionate love, not to get distracted by performing showy acts of hospitality that left me feeling like a hostess, rather than a person at home with friends. I would stick to the advice of my aikido teacher: power felt is power wasted. If I was doing something hard, I wanted it to be only because it was useful, not because I was enjoying the feeling of *how hard I was trying*.

That set one kind of limit on my first few attempts to open my home, but I wanted to add one more. There were plenty of things I could try that were hard and genuinely useful but that still felt like a bad idea as an initial attempt. More than I wanted to host a single, perfect event, I wanted to find a way to make a habit of hospitality. And I figured that might mean being conservative about what I took on initially. I wanted to begin the BenOp the same way my brother had told me to begin a weightlifting habit: start small and thus avoid overexerting myself in a way that would lead me to give up.

The first time I went to the gym, my only goal for the visit was not to make it my last visit. That meant I wasn't interested in doing reps to exhaustion or finding out exactly how many machines I could take on in one visit. If anything, I tried to undershoot what I *could* lift. As long as I kept going to the weight room regularly, I would have the chance to ramp up my sets. But it would profit me nothing to do something really impressive on day one and then be too sore and miserable ever to go back for day two.

I can be a little more profligate in prayer and hospitality than it makes sense to be in physical disciplines. No act of love, offered for God, is ever wasted (the way a single, habit-killing workout may be). God can give me the grace to do much more than I think is possible, but it can require silence, contemplation, and discernment to figure out *what* difficult thing He may be asking me to do. While I listen for His guidance on the big things, I still want to do the simpler acts of service I see before me.

Making My Little Way

So, to plan some of my first events, I thought about everything I *disliked* about asking people over and tried to eliminate each complication that made me feel unhappy about opening my home. For example, Gathering Number Ten might be the one where I learned cheerfully to offer up washing thirty plates by hand as a sacrifice, but for Gathering Number One, we would use paper plates. (And, as it happened, I've used disposable dishes for every single gathering of more than ten people I've hosted to date.)

The first event I planned was simply a meal, plus prayer and social time. I was going to be hosting twenty to thirty people for a Friday dinner. I made sure not to promise too much for the event: I told everyone that we would pray Evening Office together, share dinner, and then just enjoy each other's company until nine or nine thirty. We would wrap up with Night Office, and then I would bring out dessert. From then on, there would be no agenda besides enjoying each other's company until folks trickled out and headed home. I figured that Evening and Night Office, parts of the Liturgy of the Hours that vowed religious and many lay Catholics pray every day, would be a good way to connect our little group to the prayer of the whole Body of Christ.

It wasn't that different from the events my friends threw in non-BenOp contexts. The main difference (aside from prayer) was that I hoped the whole thing would have a greater sense of restfulness. That meant no background music and a proper cooked dinner (as opposed to pizza and chips); I was making the kind of food you couldn't eat standing up.

With just the addition of prayer and the subtraction of a kind of frantic energy, I hoped that the event might still have a markedly different character. I thought that bringing together a bunch of Christians who had come to spend time with other Christians might reshape what our small talk would be like. We could talk about a homily one of us had heard or spiritual reading or any part of our prayer life without worrying about excluding someone who thought that kind of God-talk was weird. And even if we were discussing secular matters (the latest Marvel movie, the perennial disasters in the D.C. subway system), it might still feel more natural to respond with "I'll pray for you" or even to pray together right that second, or to pass on a piece of advice we had drawn from a Christian source.

Since I'm prone to micromanagement, however, I had to resolve firmly to let the conversations move that way (or any which way) on their own, without my prompting. Having given up conversation moderation, I only had one job for the event: preparing the food. For some people, the easiest way to feed a large group might have been to make the evening a potluck, but, for me, coordinating a potluck seemed at least as stressful, if not more so, as having to wash dishes for thirty people. I knew I would feel bad bothering people to sign up to make food, and I would be dreading that at least one major dish might fall through and I would be scrambling that day to figure out how to cover gaps. For me, prone to Martha of Bethany's anxieties, it was a lot less nerve-racking to plan to do a lot of work, solo, in exchange for getting to know *exactly* how much work I would need to do and being able to schedule it accordingly.

I planned to cook, rather than order in, because I wanted to cook. (If you would rather order in, don't worry: you can still have a warm event; just make sure that the cost of prepared food won't be a strain on you or your guests, and let them know whether they're supposed to chip in. And think about what acts of hospitality, besides cooking, will help you feel that you're taking care of your guests as an act of love.) I take a lot more pleasure in cooking for others than in making meals just for myself, so taking on the task of making dinner felt as if it freed me to make something particularly yummy. I also had an ace up my sleeve: I was working at that time as a journalist, and my employer, in order to keep my weekly hours under thirty (and thus keep the company off the hook for my health insurance), had me working Monday through Thursday. With my Fridays off, I was able to take on a big cooking project without feeling rushed (and with plenty of time to take breaks).

To split up my work, I made chocolate-chip-cookie dough earlier in the week, and let it rest in the fridge until Friday.[3] Then all I had to do was pop the (preshaped) dough into the oven, and I could serve freshly baked cookies with almost no preparation work that night. The dinner was a pasta dish with asparagus, onions, breadcrumbs, and roasted tomatoes.[4] I picked the dish because I

[3] David Leite, "Perfection? Hint: It's Warm and Has a Secret", *New York Times*, July 9, 2008, http://www.nytimes.com/2008/07/09/dining/09chip.html.

[4] Tristyn Bloom, "Spinach pasta with asparagus, roasted tomatoes, and toasted breadcrumbs", *Don't Blame the Gin* (blog), January 21, 2015, https://tkbloom.tumblr.com/post/108777771397/spinach-pasta-with-asparagus-roasted-tomatoes.

really enjoyed it and because no step of the recipe was too
hard (or too sensitive to timing). I just stuck the tomatoes
in the oven, boiled the pasta, and used every remaining
burner on the stove to sauté the vegetables. It got farcical
only when I had more pasta than I had serving dishes,
so I charged the first few attendees with helping me to
redistribute pasta into cake pans. I also made a salad, but
I didn't feel as if that part of my cooking paid off, so, for
every dinner that followed, I just made an entree and
a dessert. I told my friends that there was no need to
bring anything but that if anyone wanted to bring food,
fresh fruit would be most appreciated. I set the fruit out
as starters.

Once the food was made, I tried to step out of the hostess role. I was still the hostess insofar as I was the one who
knew where the bathroom and the extra folding chairs
were, but even that became less important after the first
dinner. I tried to shift out of a management mind-set and
just appreciate seeing my friends, as happily and as simply
as I would have if I were at someone else's house. I was off
the clock until the last prayers had been said and the last
few people headed out.

At the end of the BenOp nights, I would wave off offers
to help with what dishes needed washing (usually just cups
and forks, thanks to the disposable plates). I wasn't being
generous to my guests by sparing them cleanup work; this
was part of making hosting as pleasant as possible for *me*. I
prefer to clean up alone.

There can be something very jolly about working
together to clean up, not to mention something humble
about accepting help in your own home, but I'm not very
good at either of these. I have trouble letting go of the
feeling of hostessing if people help me wash up; I put pressure on myself to make their cleaning a good experience.

Accepting help from others and stepping back from being in charge is hard for me. (My husband has, more than once, heard a clatter or a yell and run in to find me struggling to move something that would be a lot easier as a two-man job.) I've tried to accept *some* of the invitations God gives me to work on this fault (and to ask Him to keep granting me these opportunities, along with the humility to take them). I know it might sound like a good idea for me to work on this vice over a series of BenOp dinners, but, again, for the very first of those dinners, I wanted to start easy.

So, I kicked everyone out when the night came to a close and just sat down to rest for about fifteen minutes. Then, completely alone, I put on the cast recording from a musical and loudly sang along while washing up. Planning how *you* will end the evening of hosting is as important as thinking about how to make your guests' last experience of the party warm and welcoming. I liked best to be alone, not to be rushed (I had to finish cleaning before bed, but I could take breaks, which I would not do with guests), and to be a little silly and loud after a night of hosting.

But, as I write this, I notice one thing I habitually leave out of my post-event time: prayer. I made sure my guests and I prayed as the last thing we did as a group, but, once the official event wrapped up, I tended to act as though I had ushered God out along with all the departing guests. I didn't make prayer a part of my own ending ritual.

I don't know whether I would be equal to reciting a whole Rosary, at least not to start with, but the next time I host an event, I'm going to try to spend one more moment with God, once I'm "done", even if it's just praying the Trisagion (repeating three times: "Holy God, Holy Mighty One, Holy Immortal One, have mercy on us") or sitting down and pulling up a hymn I like on YouTube and singing along, or just quietly receiving it and adding an amen. I like to have "my" time, but it would be good to remember from Whom that time comes.

Going Beyond the Little Ways

Your first event should be whatever feels easiest and most exciting to you. And maybe your first couple of parties should all be squarely in your comfort zone—giving you and your guests a little stability and space to grow comfortable with each other. But when should you and your community go on to more ambitious ideas? I'm often guided by a piece of advice I got in a totally different context, when I started working on my first book. A novelist told me that the trick is not to write your story starting at the beginning of the plot and keep going until you reach the end. Instead, write all the scenes that you're excited about writing *first*. Keep doing that until you have only the boring, necessary scenes left. Then: *don't write the boring scenes at all*—not even if they're necessary to the plot. If writing them bores you, why would you expect reading them not to bore the reader? Rework the whole structure of the book, if necessary, to avoid writing anything you don't enjoy.

If *fiction* writers should free themselves that way, I could certainly allow myself the same freedom as a nonfiction writer. I could be moved by love and enthusiasm, rather than by duty. And I am even freer as a host. There's no reason for my friends to expect events at my house to form a consistent *oeuvre*. I could skip the boring parts and plan only events that delight me.

That's not to say that there aren't useful kinds of service that are boring or otherwise difficult, but I try not to think of these too much as part of my BenOp community work—not unless I can do them out of love. There are some kinds of boring work that I can (sort of) joyfully take on, such as clearing out the trash after events. It's easier for me to embrace work that makes it possible to have people over for an event I'm excited about. The boring tasks I avoid are hosting events that I can't get excited about attending. It might be nice for our BenOp group to have a board-games night, but, since I don't like playing them much myself, I would be taking on the hosting purely out of duty. I might attend this kind of event to support a friend, but I don't want to build my role in the community around events I don't enjoy attending.

Where there is a genuine need, I find it easier to ask for (and to receive) the grace from God to cope with what's asked of me. For a long time, one of the things that scared me most about one day being a parent was the fear that my kids would get sick and throw up, and I would have to clean it up, but it would be too disgusting to grapple with. (I wasn't quite sure what would happen after my failure to do the necessary thing. Would we move? Burn down the house?) But, in college, my boyfriend got a horrible stomach bug, and I found out that, although vomiting was still gross, I just plain cared a lot more about taking care of *him* than I did about fleeing the ickiness.

It's in between needs where I have trouble, when something might be generous *and* hard *and* not the obvious thing love calls for. I struggle to discern whether a big lift is a prudential choice I could take or leave or a gift God is giving me to kindle my dependence on Him. I hope that, through prayer and through *sometimes* taking a chance, I'm getting better at acting out of love more often. I want God to form my will so that some of the "boring" things that are genuinely good ideas don't feel boring to me anymore. I would like to feel more the way I hope I would if Christ appeared to me and invited me more obviously to work with Him to bring about His kingdom here on earth.

Practically speaking, that means trying to learn from a lot of small choices. Where I work, we once had an extended debate over one of our company values related to growth: improve 10 percent a week. Predictably, given that this company employs nerds like me, people wanted to pin down how literally we were supposed to take this. As a weekly goal, it sounded doable, but it actually represented a staggering rate of improvement. Working 10 percent faster every week would double a person's speed within two months.

I found a better way of framing the goal. If me-right-now and me-a-week-from-now were both applying for my job, my goal was for me-a-week-from-now to be the better candidate. I thought about the 10 percent growth target as a way of saying that there should be a perceptible difference between me and the me I was growing into.

That can also be the case for the way I offer hospitality to others. It's not the kind of thing I would want to track with such a numbers-focused or Pelagian mind-set, but over time, I am trying and praying to be better at this. And one of the most likely ways of getting better at it is by just inviting people over, trying to love them, and trying to receive the love they offer me. Taking on small projects (including the not-so-small project of working to sustain this love) can be prudent. Growing slowly and steadily means not overtaxing myself and burning out; it also means delegating some of my more ambitious ideas to my future self, who, God willing, will be better prepared to take them on. When I think about delegating these bigger projects to future me, rather than just thinking about postponing them, I have a better chance of (eventually) making these plans come to fruition. Thinking about delegating to myself makes me think about how I'll need to change to be able to take on the project: Am I just waiting till I have more time? Is there a practical skill I need to learn? Do I need to curb a particular sin or strengthen a virtue? How will the me who could take this on differ from the present me, who is struggling?

Growing as a Christian isn't the same kind of task as growing as an employee at my company. It's more obvious that I should rely on God for guidance when my problem is "How do I love Your people?" rather than "How do I classify these invoices?" But I don't mean to sell Him short. Along with all my more secular goals at my job (such as to keep clear notes for my co-workers to reference), I keep adding "Pray for the people I do tasks for." I'm in charge of running payroll, and the main thing preventing *that* from being an act of hospitality is my attitude about it. I keep trying to remember to pray for my co-workers when I pay them.

I have trouble thinking of my job as tenderly taking care of the people I work with; instead, I tend to think of it as efficiently eliminating tasks on my to-do list (some of which happen to involve people). At a performance review, I decided to take a chance and mention to my boss when we were brainstorming 10 percent growth strategies that I thought I should pray more at work. He was all for it.

The Limits of the Little Way

It doesn't take much more than a willingness to pray together to create a Benedict Option community. Theo,

an Eastern Orthodox man, wrote to Rod Dreher to share
the story of his BenOp group, which started about as small
as you could get. Theo wrote:

> Nine months ago my youngest brother was going through
> some difficulties with his faith, and we decided to meet
> on a weekly basis to explore his experience further and
> to encourage each other to stay on the path. Within a
> month, our meetings swelled into a group of fifteen guys
> (friends and relatives) with regular meetings occurring in
> my garage ever since. Over the summer we met weekly,
> we now meet fortnightly.... The meetings we have nick-
> named God's Garage. The meetings start at 9 P.M. and fin-
> ish when people have had enough, usually 2–3 A.M. Any
> discussion about God can go on forever, and that is why I
> think the meetings work well.[5]

Theo already saw these men regularly, but, out of
habit, they had talked about football, not about God and
their spiritual lives. His brother's troubles kick-started the
group, and the needs of all the men attending and the little
liturgies of their regular gatherings helped to keep it going.
Theo noted in his e-mail to Dreher that he and his friends
kept their meetings in the garage (away from their usual
hangouts). They sacralized the space by reserving it for
big questions.

This is the kind of space that anyone can clear in his life
(and in the lives of his friends). It's a space you can make
if you already have a number of Christian friends and
lack only a way to be Christian with each other. There's
just one thing that I think small, close-knit groups of

[5] Theo, e-mail quoted in Rod Dreher, "God's Garage", *American Conser-*
vative, May 15, 2017, http://www.theamericanconservative.com/dreher/gods
-garage/.

this type should be wary of. When friends get together and talk about God or spiritual life, there's always the possibility that a private charism, personal enthusiasm, or even inadvertent error can spread through the group. It is good for me to share with my friends that I like to pray the Rosary on the subway, but it is too much for me to start arguing that it is a necessary form of evangelization or worship. An attendee of a fellowship group might pass on, in a spirit of charity and fraternal correction, severe cautions on a near occasion of sin without mentioning that the priest who warned him against it was concerned with the penitent's *personal* weaknesses. By turning pastoral counsel into a universal prohibition, he misleads the others, engendering scrupulosity.

Private prayer fellowships are amplifiers, but they aren't always choosy about what is amplified. When a group takes an interest in a preacher, a discipline, an apparition, or anything else, the host (and others) should make sure that members of the group remain rooted in the Church institutionally and have a trusted spiritual confidant outside the group.

Whether that confidant is a spiritual director, a trusted pastor, a friendly nun, or a scholarly layman, the main thing is to find someone outside the group to serve as a reliable touchstone. This person can help members of the group distinguish between what draws them closer to the group *and* to God and what binds them only to the group. It may be helpful to invite some of these outside friends to meetings occasionally, so they can be a moderating influence or speak to you afterward if they think the group is getting diverted from God.

This kind of error is easy for well-meaning, faithful friends to draw each other into. Even those who have done great good are not proof against this danger. Kate

Hennessy, the granddaughter of Dorothy Day, explains in *Dorothy Day: The World Will Be Saved by Beauty: An Intimate Portrait of My Grandmother* why she believes that her grandmother made an error of this kind when organizing retreats for the Catholic Worker movement.

Day heard Father Pacifique Roy preach and found his spirituality moving and convicting. She booked him to speak at a retreat that Catholic Worker members were encouraged to attend. And she kept bringing him back to preach, even though, in Hennessy's telling (based on interviews with her mother and other Workers), many of Day's friends found that Roy's sermons left them feeling hopeless. His emphasis on putting aside all comforts—even friendship—as distractions from God didn't sound like the community they joined. Even after Father Roy's superior forbade him to conduct any more retreats (which lends weight to the misgivings of other Catholic Workers), Day kept seeking an exception, hoping to hear him again and to share his preaching with others.

Any group can make Day's mistake. The greater the intimacy that builds up between you and your friends, the greater potential you have to serve each other, but greater also is the potential to become oriented around a *piece* of the gospel or spiritual life instead of the whole. In addition to keeping connections to people and events outside your group, it can help to treasure your crotchety friends or the ones who don't want to go too far—they can help someone else in your circle feel freer to speak up if he has a problem. The less your group does, the less of a problem this will be. If you get together for dinner and Evening Office every now and then, there's a small good being accomplished and a small risk of harm. If you focus deeply on one teacher or practice, be more attentive to this danger.

When the Little Way Feels Impossible

When I run into problems in my community, I find I'm far less often stymied by tensions within the group than by ones within myself. When I try to plan an event, it's easy for brainstorming to slide into catastrophizing: "Maybe no one will come." "Maybe everyone will be bored." "Maybe I'm just not charismatic enough to pull this off." And the more I dwell on these thoughts, the more they start to feel like experiences I've already had. It's easy to learn cowardice from daydreams.

It helps me to have small, clear successes to look back on, as an answer to those imagined failures. Easy events I've already held give me the gumption to try more ambitious ideas (and to believe that my friends will forgive me if tonight's plan falls through). Even baking before events acts as a small step in a success spiral (a sequence of small successes that creates a feeling of increasing momentum and strength). Before anyone comes over, I've already had a small, incontrovertible victory. And, at least in my case, acts such as baking and building do the most to buoy my spirits. A kindly written e-mail may do good, but it's not as solidly there as a cooling batch of cookies or a repaired couch (mine collapsed during a too-well-attended Shakespeare reading). Self-doubt can nibble away at an intangible achievement, but it's much harder for it to make light of a concrete one.

I also keep in mind (although I sometimes have to talk myself into it) that self-doubt can be a result of spiritual warfare, and I might want to respond to it as such. The running monologue that keeps telling you, "I can't" is called "negative self-talk" or "intrusive thoughts" by cognitive scientists. But Eastern Orthodox theologians have a different word for them: *logismoi*. *Logismoi* are any repeated thoughts that we let become part of ourselves and hold us at a distance from God.

For a long while after my conversion, I was troubled by a persistent *logismos*: "You're too bad at praying to be a Christian." Reading Kyriacos C. Markides' *Mountain of Silence: A Search for Orthodox Spirituality* helped me to put a name to this kind of temptation. It was easier for me to resist a *logismos* when I knew it was part of a pattern of spiritual attack, not the revelation of a fatal flaw in myself.

Of course, if I'm having doubts about party planning, it's not necessarily a sign that Satan is standing in my way! If I'm worried about how I can feed thirty people when fifteen of those people didn't RSVP until the morning of the event, that's a pretty reasonable worry. If my husband and I have been thoughtless about our schedules and booked ourselves to travel for five weekends in a row, it's completely unsurprising that the thought of hosting anyone the first week we're finally free makes us feel exhausted.

But if you're thinking of doing something that seems possible for *someone else* in your situation but seems impossible only for *you*, consider turning to Saint Michael to intercede for you against external oppression before you assume that you're one of Saint Jude's lost causes. Hospitality isn't low stakes: we're called to love each other actively. The Letter to the Hebrews tells us that hospitality opens the door not just to our fellow man but to heaven itself: "Do not neglect to show hospitality to strangers, for thereby some have entertained angels unawares" (13:2).

I keep in my living room an icon of Rublev's *Hospitality of the Trinity* (which shows the angels whom Abraham entertained unawares) to remind my guests and me of what we are doing when we come together. Getting together with other Christians to care for each other and strengthen our faith is exactly the kind of thing that the prince of this world would want to thwart. Scones and tea may seem like silly weapons in spiritual warfare, but they can be potent. If you feel as if you're getting crushed when you try to offer them to others, it might be because you're dangerous (in the best way).

5

"Go and Do Likewise"
(A Cheat Sheet of Events)

If you're interested in the little way of the Benedict Option—taking on small projects now and figuring out the big picture later, once you and your friends have built a foundation of small acts of hospitality and love—now might be a good time to put this book down, say a prayer, and pick a date to gather your friends. Here are some tips for gathering two or three in His name, including some ways to make it easy on yourself, if cooking, hosting, and talking aren't really to your taste.

Don't want to cook? Whenever I want to have people over, but don't have time or don't want to prepare much in the way of food, I schedule the event to start somewhere between two and three o'clock on a Saturday or Sunday afternoon. It's late enough to assume that everyone has already eaten lunch and early enough to let you wrap up before people have a reason to wonder if you'll have dinner for them. (I sometimes mention the anticipated end time explicitly in my invitations, so people can make dinner plans accordingly.)

When I schedule these weekend events, I often bake cookies, because I *like* baking cookies, but any small snack will cover you. My favorite store-bought solution is a

bunch of grapes, which are tasty yet not likely to be mind-
lessly inhaled, like chips.

These afternoon events can flow pretty easily into
"Let's all go out for dinner" if you and your guests don't
want to end the get-together at five o'clock (and if you,
as the host, don't want to have to start cooking suddenly
or to let everyone order pizza and stay in your house
indefinitely). But keep in mind that, especially if some
of your friends are recent graduates or have low-paying
jobs, eating out may break their budgets. They'll feel left
out when the party keeps going without them, especially
if it becomes the traditional end to your events. I've tried
to prevent this from happening too often at my events,
and my friends' busyness has been my ally. Usually, about
half the attendees *can't* stay out too much later, so it's easier to make an exit if you're constrained by money rather
than time. As long as restaurant outings don't happen too
often, and don't sweep up enough people to make the
outings feel like part of the events proper, I don't worry
too much.

Don't want to host an event in your home? One thing
I miss most about college is the easy access to space for
events. My alma mater had common rooms in each resi-
dential college, dining halls, study rooms in the libraries,
lawns on the quads, and plain old unlocked classrooms.
Some of these spaces we officially reserved; some we just
squatted in until we were kicked out; and, for one location, we propped open a little-used door at the top of a fire
escape during the day, reentered that night after the building was closed, climbed onto a desk to reach the trapdoor
that led to the roof ... You get the idea.

But once I graduated, there weren't public spaces that
were easy to use (and trespassing laws were a bit more

likely to be enforced). I've been shushed in public libraries for talking too much to my husband. And, eventually, a concierge will realize that neither you nor any of your friends are staying in the hotel in whose atrium you've been hanging out. By default, Starbucks and other coffee shops play host to one-on-one meetings, but they're not a good fit for hosting a cheerful crowd.

Sometimes I ask a friend who is still in college or graduate school to get us back into the world of semipublic, multiuse spaces. But, in the absence of folks who can sneak us onto campus, my best plan is usually to meet in a park. Parks (especially large parks) allow you to invite a fairly big group without inconveniencing other patrons. And parks make it easy to split your group for different activities or conversations, since you're not confined to a single room.

Unfortunately, meeting in a park makes my plans weather dependent. I must also make sure that the location works for any friends with mobility issues. I have one friend who uses a wheelchair, and other friends seem to take turns spraining ankles or breaking feet (I've done both). Parks may also mean limited access to bathrooms. And they may diminish your friends' interest in doing anything too strange or noisy. A heavily trafficked park may or may not feel like the right place to sing hymns lustily, for example.

Don't want to do too much to *run* the event? There are plenty of nourishing events that don't require a lot of active work from the host. All you may need to do is announce a time and place and then step back. You can lend your home for an event and let someone else take on the work of hosting it. When I lived in D.C., my apartment was better located than many of my friends' homes, and I made sure folks knew that I was sometimes willing to lend my living room to people who needed a place to hold an event. That's how I wound up hosting a going-away party for a friend who was moving to England and a monthly Narnia book club. My friends did all the planning and hosting (running the dates by me in advance), and I got to enjoy the events as a guest—with no commute!

I've also enjoyed running events that mostly run themselves. My husband and I threw a poetry-recitation party, for which all we had to do was make dinner and memorize one poem apiece. The evening really took care of itself as we all took turns reciting a poem that was meaningful to us. A few months later, I scheduled a litany-of-saints picnic, hoping to have a similar experience. I wanted it to be an informal show-and-tell, in which my friends would say something about saints who had shaped their lives. For the poetry event, we asked our guests to come with at least one poem memorized, but for the saints event we requested no advance preparation; the sharing was impromptu. (And I didn't have to prepare anything as the host either—we were in a park, eating whatever snacks guests brought to share.)

I asked our guests to tell us about a single moment in the lives of their saints, or a moment when a saint touched *their* lives, or to share with us a prayer associated with that saint. If two people wanted to talk about the same saint, no problem! Each would talk about his own love for the saint, so there was little danger of overlap. I wasn't looking for book reports or birth-to-death hagiographies. I just wanted my friends to tell me whatever they found most electrifying about a saint. ("Catherine of Siena scares me." "Here's how I started wearing a Miraculous Medal." "No, *my* Saint Christina isn't 'the Astonishing', but ..." "I thought Saint Thérèse of Liseux was a little treacly, until ..." "I picked my confirmation saint for his faults, not his virtues.") Before we parted ways, we prayed a litany of the saints, including all the saints we had introduced to each other.

I've come to love many saints because of friends who were generous in sharing the saints they encountered. One of my friends, Jenna Andrews, is a positive Rolodex of saints, and she always introduced me to them with an infectious joy. I wanted to hold a litany-of-saints event so that I could catch that kind of contagious joy from more of my friends (especially as Jenna had since moved away, joined the Hawthorne Dominicans, and now cares for the dying as Sister Diana Marie).

Our poetry night and the saints event were both mixtape parties. There was little for me to do as host except name the theme of the mixtape and let everyone loose. (My friend Sarah got the closest to a literal mixtape party when she hosted a hymn sing-along.) The easiest way to come up with a mixtape party theme is to think of something you love learning about from others and then invite all your friends over to tell stories.

Don't want to be responsible for anything, but still want to have an event? It's okay to cheat—just piggyback off an event that's already happening. Many cities have a number of groups that bring interesting speakers to town (authors at bookstores, open-to-the-public lectures at universities, Theology on Tap events, etc.). There are also opportunities to center your event in worship. You might invite friends to join you for Adoration after work and then all go out to dinner afterward (or brown-bag it and head to a park or a plaza). You can invite friends to accompany you to any kind of organized event, but it may be best to pick something you've never done before (either individually or as part of a group). That way, you'll get to try something new, and the event will feel a little rarer and more enticing.

Keep an eye on your church's bulletin (and ask your friends to watch theirs) to see if there's an interesting litany, a lessons and carols service, or a special prayer service you might all like to attend together. An Eastern Orthodox friend invited us to his parish's Bridegroom Matins during the first half of Holy Week.

Another simple option is to find a church that keeps its doors unlocked and to meet there to pray for a particular intention (a safe delivery for a friend whose baby is due soon, healing for a friend who is sick, a reawakening of faith for a family member who has left the Church, hope for a friend who is looking for work, or anything else that seems urgent). I recommend a prayer that feels specific and urgent, rather than perennial (such as "an end to all wars"), so that the friends you're inviting to join you feel less inclined to think that they could pray for this intention at any time. Once you've gathered, you can pray a Rosary, a chaplet, or a litany that fits the intention that you've gathered for. Allow some time for silent contemplation.

At the end of your prayer, linger in each other's company for a little while. You can go out for food or coffee, take a walk together, or head to a public area with seating. Take a little time just to rejoice in the foretaste of heaven that your small communion has revealed. And give God the chance to give you any other promptings about how to love each other, after you've spent some time listening to Him together.

6

Doing Together What You Do Alone

The little way of small, comfortable community events is spiritually fruitful. If your efforts at community never grew beyond that point, you and your friends would still be bolstered by those humble ways of loving each other. When you reach beyond the efforts at community that come most naturally, the road will be bumpier. Mine certainly has been! Expect to invent and discard ideas for gathering together, as the act of extending yourself in love changes you and makes new ideas possible.

If you want to start creating community, look for examples around you to imitate or even co-opt. If free pizza attracted people in college, maybe it will keep working now that you're all (ostensibly) adults? If beguines shared their lives and had home-based trades, maybe you should take up . . . weaving. Or Etsy crafting. Or whatever is the twenty-first-century equivalent that lets people be home and ready to welcome each other during the day. Branching out from what is already working or what you know has worked in the past isn't a bad way to begin, but if you stop there, a lot that will be occluded from your view.

Richard Beck, a Christian author and professor of psychology, noticed that most Christian churches trying to build up community by creating spaces for fellowship and spontaneous gatherings seem to converge on the same solution: a coffee shop. Maybe they have an actual shop, complete with espresso machines, set up in their church complex, or maybe they rent a storefront and use coffee as a lure to get "seekers" to enter a less churchy space where they might have a chance to be exposed to the gospel message. Although Beck approved of the impulse to create shared places for the community, he had trouble believing that a coffee shop was the model that churches should be imitating.

The trouble was, the stores that churches were using as a blueprint were pretty narrowly targeted. Beck wrote, "Coffee shops tend to be a part of affluent White culture. The working poor don't hang out in coffee shops with their Mac laptops. Nor can they afford $4 specialty drinks."[1] Considering the needs of his own church's members in Abilene, Texas, and the needs of their surrounding community, he thought it would make more sense for his church to open a laundromat.

The laundromats in his community served the working poor, but they served them poorly. The facilities were dirty, the English-only signs left Spanish speakers confused, and nothing about the places was welcoming—even though the businesses expected that patrons would wait in the laundromat for more than an hour, keeping watch over their clothes. Beck hoped that his parish could meet this genuine need with more warmth and joy than the local businesses managed to muster. And, thanks to his blogging, one of the members of his church did just that.

---

[1] Richard Beck, "Instead of a Coffee Shop How About a Laundromat?", *Experimental Theology* (blog), February 9, 2015, http://experimentaltheology .blogspot.com/2015/02/instead-of-coffee-shop-how-about.html.

Wash This Way opened in 2017 and is treating its patrons with dignity and kindness.[2]

When I tried to identify BenOp projects to work on or reasons I might open up my home, I tried to remember Beck's example and to look for a genuine need I could meet, especially an undeserved need. I wanted to avoid taking on only projects I was sure would succeed but might be of limited relevance. That meant I didn't care so much about book discussions or speaker series, already well covered by churches, bookstores, and other Catholic groups in the city. I wanted at least some ideas that were more a work of mercy than a party.

Unfortunately, I can't say that I'm a very astute observer of others' needs. I'm trying to get better, and I'm still hoping that BenOp ties will make it easier for friends to ask for my help (and vice versa). But, especially as I began my BenOp endeavors, I figured one of the easiest ways for me to make sure I was addressing a *real* need was to think of my own needs.

Ora et Labora et Cookies

Beck's idea for a laundromat was a great project because it intervened at a moment when people were being made to feel small and valueless. As a Christian, I think that anything that makes people feel worthless is bad, not just because the people feel bad, or because it's bad for their self-esteem, but because it's a *lie*. As a Christian, I *know* that everyone is a child of God, intended for sainthood,

[2] Richard Beck, "Wash This Way: Instead of a Coffee Shop How About a Laundromat?", *Experimental Theology* (blog), April 5, 2017, http://experimental theology.blogspot.com/2017/04/wash-this-way-instead-of-coffee-shop.html.

someone for whom Christ willingly died on the cross. Making people feel worthless (intentionally or not) is an anti-gospel. Attacking that lie is a way to proclaim the gospel and defy the devil.

So, I asked myself, when did *I* feel worthless?

I tend to feel most awful about myself whenever I have to apply for a new job. During one of the worst periods, I was applying for journalism jobs, which, due to high demand, could get away with not really being jobs at all, but internships for entry-level positions. These internships paid nothing to almost nothing. I applied for job after job and frequently heard nothing in reply to my cover letters. The companies I was contacting valued my work so little that they didn't even want to chat on the phone with me to find out whether they would like my full-time work for free. Economically speaking, I was worth less than nothing to them.

I had to psych myself up to work on applications or work on them only during brief scheduled times, trying to keep the ugliness from spilling over into the rest of my day. Sometimes I would work on cover letters while listening to the cast album of *Sweeney Todd* (a show about a murderous barber) or a playlist a friend of mine had put together, titled "The Futility of All Human Ambition, as Expressed by Musicals". It was hard not to write the applications in a fatalist or despairing mood (which probably didn't help my chances).

As my friends and I were kicking off the BenOp project, I had recently started a new job and had no plans to be applying again soon, but I had plenty of friends who were between jobs, planning to change jobs, or staring down the end of an internship. I knew my friends were looking for jobs, sometimes because I saw their posts on Facebook asking for leads and sometimes because they asked me to edit their cover letters. But, as far as I knew, they were working on their applications the same way I had: alone and in a black mood.

What would it take to give the lie to the feelings of worthlessness that had crushed me? I wanted to pierce the feeling of abandonment and powerlessness, so I invited my job-seeking friends over to work, pray, and eat—but not in that order.

My friends came over, laptops in hand, and we started by praying Evening Office together. Even if the point of the event was to get work done, I wanted to start with prayer, to give my friends a fighting chance of remembering God and that He loves us, before we were all reminded that employers didn't. Then, while I worked on dinner, everyone in turn named the task he planned to work on for the next twenty minutes, and I set a timer. Every twenty minutes, my friends took a short break, updated the room on what they had done, received high fives, and named a task (which could be continuing their first task) for the next twenty minutes.

After about an hour's worth of work cycles, we took a break to eat, praying the blessing over our meal together. Our only job during dinner was to enjoy each other's company. Once we had finished, my friends did another hour or hour and a half of twenty-minute work cycles, while I made a skillet-size cookie for us to share for dessert. Throughout the event, if I wasn't at a fiddly step of a recipe, I was around to read letters (and so was anyone else who wanted to spend a work cycle taking a breather from his own project).

I broke the work time into small bursts because I had found this approach (often referred to as the Pomodoro Technique) helpful in my own work, especially for the work I least wanted to do. The Pomodoro cycles helped me to stay focused, but they also helped by limiting how discouraged any task could make me. If I started on an open-ended project with "as long as it takes to finish" hanging over me, it was hard not to fear that I would spend the rest of the night being miserable. But when I forced myself to take breaks and to choose whether to keep working, I knew that, in the worst-case scenario, I would be miserable for a maximum of twenty minutes. And then I could read a novel or pray or listen to music or do anything else that felt more nourishing than figuring out what comes after "I am applying for the position of ..." (I shortened the recommended length of Pomodoro cycles—they're twenty-five minutes by default—because twenty-five minutes of misery felt like too much to take on, but I could bring myself to do twenty.)

I wanted my friends to have respites from their work, the chance to be happy about any progress they had made, and the opportunity to decide to stop if they couldn't continue working without being pulled into despair. After the end of the second set of work cycles, I took the skillet cookie out of the oven, and we ate it together. Finally, we ended the night by praying Night Office together. The two prayers from the Divine Office enclosed our time together, tucking it inside prayer—specifically, a prayer that is shared throughout the Church. Our work might leave us lonely, but our prayer connected us to Catholics across the world who were all praying these same psalms together.

This is an event I plan to repeat, and I know one thing I would like to change the next time I try it. The first time, I assigned all the cooking tasks to myself. I picked recipes that were easy to accomplish solo, and I worked alone while my friends worked on their applications. I reasoned that it was part of hospitality to make my friends feel taken care of (and to avoid visibly not working on job applications myself). But I wonder if it would have been a better bulwark against hopelessness if I had made pizza dough and had all my friends prep and assemble the toppings.

Although I was trying to cook to show my friends how much I valued them, I didn't give them a chance to be useful themselves. The work they were doing was, by its nature, disconnected from the fruits of their labor (send an application now, maybe get a reply sometime next month). It might have been a gift to let them be immediately useful in the way that cooking always is. It's hard for me to step out of the role of host and organizer and to realize that I might be standing in the way of grace.

Only three people came to that event. It was the smallest event I've ever organized. But I think it was one of the most successful, because it was particularly needed by those friends.

What Do You Do Alone That You Could Do Together?

I tried to follow Beck's example and look for real needs I could meet, not just weakly successful ideas I could imitate. And another question I asked myself helped me to plan BenOp projects: What do you do alone that you could do together? My jobs gathering had fallen into this category: we had lessened the misery of this kind of work by doing it together. We could offer a visible contradiction to those *logismoi* of "No one wants you", "You're worthless" that crept in during the work of being rejected again and again.

A lot of the wishes that my friends had expressed at our first BenOp brainstorming event were things like my job-application event. Well, nearly: my friends didn't ask as often for solidarity in the midst of misery, but for opportunities to share joy. My friends wanted to go to Adoration, to sing, to visit the Franciscan Monastery of the Holy Land Friars, but not all by themselves! These were all things we could do alone but longed to do together.

As Christians, we need to cultivate habits of silence and contemplation. It would be much better if I didn't have such a hard time being still in front of Christ in the Eucharist. One way I could try to address this failing would be to rebalance my prayer life: I could give up some group activities to get the right proportions of silent and social worship. But that would mean pruning the vibrant part of my spiritual life, instead of using the prayers I find most natural as a way to ask for help with the stunted ones. I would rather take a both-and approach, looking for chances to worship more with friends *and* to spend more time with God alone. If your balance of active and contemplative worship feels off to you, do more of what is missing, rather than less of what you are doing.

One of my BenOp friends organized a hymn sing at her house. She (and another talented attendee) played piano, and we all picked favorite hymns to sing. We got the chance to learn each other's favorites and why our friends were moved by those songs. It was another one of our small events (four or five people), but it was something I had wished for, for a long time.

One year, I had gone Christmas caroling in the city with a group of friends, nearly half of whom sang in professional choirs (I was in the other half). We had great fun standing by subway entrances and singing in four-part harmony, but the organizers objected when a few of the amateurs wanted to take on songs for which we didn't have sheet music broken out by soprano, alto, tenor, and bass. If we tried to add in songs spontaneously, they wouldn't be up to snuff. I was in the group that wanted to add music, but since this wasn't my event, I backed off after being rebuffed. *This* event was focused on beautiful, not lusty, singing.

The problem was, until my friend's hymn sing, I had trouble finding an alternative. Every year, a little too late to put plans into motion, I think about organizing friends for *Easter* caroling. But every year so far, I've been prevented by my own travel plans or I've just plain chickened out, thinking friends will be busy or will want to do it only if we can do it perfectly, with parts, rehearsals, and so forth. I don't want to give a formal concert; I just want to stand on corners and bawl out "Hail Thee, Festival Day" at the top of my lungs with a similarly excited group.

I wanted to sing Easter songs with others because my Easter Sundays keep being strangely quiet and subdued. When I go to Easter Vigil Mass on Saturday night, the liturgy is joyful and glorious. But when I get up on Sunday, it feels as if Easter is all wrapped up. Even though it's really the beginning of the Easter Octave, which means that Easter is celebrated as a solemnity for eight days in a row, it feels like an ordinary Sunday, except in one respect: it's the one Sunday in the year I'm *not* at Mass.

I entered the Church as a twenty-something convert. Perhaps people who grew up as Christians may have more Easter traditions and celebrations from their childhood that they hold on to as adults. But my friends in the city didn't seem to have Easter habits that last after the Vigil bonfire has burned out. Some traveled back to their families, as I do now that I've married into a Christian family, but the ones who were alone seemed, well, alone. In response, one of my friends hosts a brunch for "Easter orphans" who aren't headed home, but his event is meant to be broadly inclusive. Christians and non-Christians alike are welcome, so the event is light on prayer (but heavy on lamb). The Easter season lasts for fifty days; I wanted to spend more than just one of them making a joyful noise. Easter is a terrible time to feel orphaned—even in the deepest agony of His Passion, Christ entrusted us, with John, to Mary as her children. And, as brothers and sisters in Christ, we are made to take care of each other.

Whose Streets? God's Streets!

Sometimes it was enough to gather people, to share joy or sorrow in one of our homes or in church. But for some kinds of worship, it seemed *untrue* to pray privately together in my home, just as it felt *untrue* to work on job applications individually, vulnerable to despair. When we prayed quietly, sedately, at home, it felt as though prayer were something we were choosing—something we might as easily not choose. Prayer isn't gratuitous; it is natural and necessary for us and for the whole world: it is our reaction as creatures to being loved into existence by God.

When Christ entered Jerusalem, the Pharisees were appalled by the joyful shouts of His followers and asked Him to command His disciples to be silent. Christ answered them, "I tell you, if these were silent, the very stones would cry out" (Lk 19:40). Christ's words apply to our time as well. His foot does not tread upon our streets, but He is present at every Mass and carried out into the world by us, when we receive Him in the Eucharist and become living tabernacles. On some days, we carry Him out with public eucharistic processions, but every Sunday, our Shepherd is entrusted to our care. If we step out into the street after Mass and head into the subways indistinguishable from all the other Sunday-morning travelers, whose bellies are full of eggs Benedict, isn't our incognito an implicit lie?

The pressures that pinch public worship aren't all anti-Christian or even broadly anti-religious. Sociologist Ray Oldenburg hypothesizes that our culture has mistaken lively joy for a public nuisance. We confine high-spiritedness to the indoors but then wind up abolishing those refuges, too. Oldenburg laments the decline of casual gathering places such as bars, parks, stoops, and so forth, which offered people a place outside of work and home to be sociable. He sees, with their closing, a further decrease of acceptable fora for public acts of delight.

> The latitude for spirited expression in modern society is lessened. People are made nervous by it. The public pays no attention to the young man walking along with a radio blaring next to his ear nowadays, but let him sing—let him make his own music—and they're apt to frown at him. . . . The "world out there" . . . doesn't want men to dance together or gather in the local parks and sing in harmony 'round kegs of beer. That which, in a less constricted but better ordered society, is emblematic of peace and good-will, is likely to be regarded as disturbing the peace in our own. . . . The average person, popular opinion suggests, ought to be content with a little singing in the shower.[3]

If I didn't want to confine my purely *secular* singing to the shower, I certainly didn't want my worship confined to church, my home, and the inside of my head. As the nineteenth-century hymn asks, "Since Christ is Lord of heaven and earth, how can I keep from singing?" Making

---

[3] Ray Oldenburg, *The Great Good Place: Cafés, Coffee Shops, Bookstores, Bars, Hair Salons, and Other Hangouts at the Heart of a Community* (Philadelphia: Da Capo Press, 1989), 59.

a joyful noise is natural to me; making a *harmonious* noise, particularly as I tried to worship in public, has taken more trial and error. Happily, trial and error is a good way to get started. As long as you cling to God through prayer, silent adoration, and other practices of discernment, there's no reason to be afraid of taking chances to pray with others. Give God some effort to shape; do not wait for Him to prod you into action.

7

Doing Publicly What You Do Privately

Being ready to pray in public is one of the simplest ways for me to obey the will of God, as Paul explains it in his First Letter to the Thessalonians: "Rejoice always, pray constantly, give thanks in all circumstances" (5:16–18). If I'm willing to pull out my rosary on the subway, it's not all about evangelization or public witness; it's primarily opening up one more circumstance where I can pray.

But, as a convert, I had trouble feeling unselfconscious about prayer, even when I was alone. My habits were too new to feel natural. When I prayed the Sorrowful Mysteries on my commute, or even when I crossed myself while silently saying grace, I worried that I was being disruptive or obnoxious. I kept hesitating—even when I was in New York City, where my praying would almost never be the weirdest thing another commuter saw.

Part of the problem was that public prayer meant publicly identifying myself as a Christian. Once I was the girl with a rosary, it felt as if everything else I did was an act of public witness. That pressure was sometimes helpful: when I started wearing a cross necklace, I had a good reason to think twice about how I participated in the scrum on the subway platform (throwing elbows was out; darting between people was borderline). But I squirmed at the thought of being obliged to be open to conversation, rather than free to extricate myself, as I usually did when traveling.

Sometimes that responsibility was a spur to my virtue, but I still worried that being visibly at prayer would open me up to letting others down. I didn't know how well I would live up to the task of being an icon of the Church, the way habited religious are. In "Hypervisible Church", an essay in *First Things*, Catherine Addington writes, "A nun in her habit, a priest in his collar, becomes an anthropomorphic Church onto which passersby can project whatever Catholicism means to them."[1] Sometimes that means that strangers approach, asking for prayers, advice, or another kind of help. Sometimes it means people approach in anger or even with violence. Addington's piece was written in response to the martyrdom of Father Jacques Hamel, who, while offering Mass, was murdered by Islamic extremists who were looking not for him but for any priest to kill.

I didn't fear violence; what I was most scared of was the people who might not approach at all but might hate or fear the Church and, when they saw me standing in for her, would feel frightened or rejected. I was scared that if they were silently hurt, I would be deepening the wound, without the chance to try to heal it. Some of my early experiments with prayer in public left me worried that this was the effect I would have everywhere.

Praying in Mixed Company

My first problem wasn't the result of anything as dramatic as a public procession. The offending prayer didn't occur in

---

[1] Catherine Addington, "Hypervisible Church", *First Things* (July 27, 2016), https://www.firstthings.com/blogs/firstthoughts/2016/07/hypervisible -church.

public at all—just in mixed company. I had experimented with incorporating prayer into some of my non-BenOp events, gatherings that included a mix of Christians and non-Christians for movies, debates, or book clubs. One night, when we had gathered for scones and a new episode of *Sherlock*, I tried something new. The discussion of the show was winding down, people were putting on their shoes in the living room, and I said that I was going to pray Night Office in my bedroom. If folks wanted to join me before they headed out, they would be welcome.

I tried to plan ahead to lessen whatever awkwardness my invitation would create. I gave a little explanation of Night Office ("a traditional prayer to close the day"). I made sure to invite people to join me in a different room, so my non-Christian friends wouldn't feel trapped or chased out of the room. And I waited till the very end of the event to have a prayer at all, so there would be no need to wait around for the event to resume.

But I didn't succeed. One of my friends (raised Protestant but no longer practicing), let me know that she had felt pretty uncomfortable and wished I hadn't added a coda to the otherwise secular event. She told me that having prayer at the close of the event left her feeling unsure about how to make her exit: "There was this feeling: Do I leave now and say good-bye before some other people go pray Night Office? What if I want to hang out and talk to other guests or Leah? Once they're done praying, are they done for the night socially?"

I had anticipated some of these objections and could probably have addressed them by communicating better. But my friend had felt more than disoriented; the addition of Night Office left her feeling hurt. She told me later that it felt to her as though I were saying, "Oh, hey, heathen friends, sorry I need to abandon you all for ten minutes behind literal closed doors." What really rankled her was *my choice* to pray the Divine Office as part of the event with others, rather than waiting until everyone left.

I wasn't a nun or a tertiary of a religious order who had made a promise to say these prayers. If I had had a religious obligation to pray at that specific moment, she would have felt more accommodating, but, in her view, if it wasn't mandatory, it was willful. Religion was something she knew how to make space for if it was an obligation. If I weren't making a choice, she could be patient, because I wouldn't be culpable for the inconvenience. But if I chose to pray because I *wanted* to, not because I had to, she felt I was choosing God over my guests.

I wasn't so sure how to answer this objection, because it was true, at least a little bit. When I pray at events, I'm trying to choose God *and* my guests, but that "and" feels like a stretch to friends who don't share my belief. At best, I may seem rude, like someone who takes a nonurgent phone call in the middle of a conversation. At worst, I may seem pushy, like a friend who invites you over for what you thought was a social call but is actually a hard sell for a product.

I don't want my friends to feel ignored or abused, but there's another wrong I'm trying to avoid, too. I don't think I'm treating my guests well if I welcome them into my home, but then, like Bluebeard, locking away the remains of his murdered wives, keep all evidence that I'm a Christian hidden away.

My friends would rightly be appalled if I kept my husband a secret, if I never spoke about or to him in public. If I excluded my friends from a relationship that was so central to my life, they would feel that they were being held at arm's length. And they would worry about my husband, too! It's almost always a bad sign for a romantic relationship if you don't want to introduce your beloved to your friends. A hothouse love can't be healthy.

My relationship with God is more fundamental to my being than my relationship with my husband, but, on social media and in person, God gets short shrift.

At present, my apartment has a fair amount of religious paraphernalia visible, so it's not as though my friends are in danger of leaving my home without any idea that I'm Catholic. (When I lived in D.C., one of my housemates had requested that there be no icons or religious art in common spaces, so they stayed on the bookcase in my bedroom. They made trips out to the living room during BenOp events, but I always put them away when the last guests left.) Having religious objects out, but not interacted with, however, still makes me feel as if something is missing. When I went to see a collection of Russian art at a museum, I wanted to break into the cases to rescue the icons and the chalices. They weren't made for looking at, but for being reverently kissed and for holding the Blood of Christ to offer to His people. Seeing them in a museum's permanent collection made me feel as if they were imprisoned.

When I hide away my devotions, my friends end up with all the opportunities to feel excluded by the fact of my love for God, without any chances to see that love *lived*.

Before I became a Christian, I often felt uncomfortable when people prayed in my presence. (Were they mad that I wasn't participating? Would they start loudly, passive-aggressively praying for my conversion?) But some of those occasions were my first chances to witness what prayer was like, rather than relying on my imagination. Night Office was one of the prayers I had first gotten to see—my friends from college debate stepped out of our long-running alumni debate around eleven at night to pray, before returning to the debate floor to keep up the fight.

My efforts at semipublic prayer are still a work in progress. What I've been trying more recently is moving prayer to the *beginning* of otherwise secular social events, rather than offering it at the end, as I did at that *Sherlock* party. When my husband and I hosted a reading of Shakespeare's *Twelfth Night* on Epiphany (the twelfth night of the Christmas season), we listed two start times on the Facebook description of our event. Before we began the play, we would be chalking our door with an abbreviation of *Christus mansionem benedicat* (May Christ bless this house) and praying the blessing that accompanies this Epiphany tradition. If anyone wanted to join us for prayer, we said, they should show up at the earlier start time. The second start time was for people who preferred to skip the prayer and join us just for the play reading. About seven people came to pray with us. A few others misjudged their travel time and arrived in the middle of the blessing.

Another time, we were planning an all-day Shakespeare marathon, during which we would watch film adaptations of parts 1, 2, and 3 of *Henry VI* and then finish the night with *Richard III*. We tried the same two-start-time approach, telling our guests that we would start making pancakes at 11 A.M., but that, for anyone who wanted to come a half hour earlier, we would be praying Morning Office. On that occasion, no one showed up for prayer! Alexi and I prayed ourselves and then headed into the kitchen to make a double batch of pancake batter.

I haven't gotten complaints about the new approach, but I'm not sure whether I'm happy about it. Announcing ahead of time that prayer will happen makes it feel *more* like an official part of the event to me. And announcing it on Facebook or by e-mail, rather than casually, in person, makes it feel as if I'm losing the chance to be contagiously joyful about prayer. In a year, I won't be surprised if I'm trying something different, encountering both new blessings and new difficulties.

How Off-Putting Is Public Prayer?

As an atheist-to-Catholic convert, I've experienced being on the outside and the inside of prayer in religiously mixed groups, and I've felt nervous on both sides. When I was present (and not praying) while Christians prayed, I usually assumed that they disliked or distrusted me. As I held back, I figured that they saw me as spoiling their event or were thinking of me as a sinner. If I had to guess how they felt about me, I would have said that at best they pitied me, and at worst they despised me.

Now that I *am* Catholic, I don't feel any of those things when I pray in the presence of non-Christians. But I don't think my atheist friends are obligated to give me the benefit of the doubt. There's enough anti-witness in the world—think of those street preachers who seem a little too excited about their enumerated lists of people going to hell—to make atheists and other non-Christians believe that Christians hate them. Little wonder that their hackles go up when suddenly the room is visibly split into Christians and non-Christians.

This conflict comes up for me most often at mealtimes. For most prayers, if I want to keep them private, it's not too difficult. I can say a Hail Mary in my head instead of out loud. I can postpone a full Chaplet of Divine Mercy for later. But the grace I say before meals involves making the sign of the cross, and it can't really be delayed until I'm alone, after the meal. It makes sense that when I ask God to bless my food, the prayer can't be a matter of thought alone. I'm asking God's blessing on my body, and the food that sustains it. It makes sense that my body is part of the act of prayer.

I could run through the theological argument for the fittingness and beauty of a physical prayer before meals, but my anxiety persisted. On and off after my conversion, I found ways to strike a silly balance between piety and politeness. I've crossed myself under the table, out of view of the other guests, and prayed silently. I've said grace in the kitchen, before I joined everyone else at the table, or anywhere else I could get a moment alone when the dinner bell rang. (The worst of these improvisations involved ducking into the bathroom.) I kept contorting myself, trying to do right, as best I could, by God *and* my friends and family. I was willing to try anything, except asking them directly how they felt.

Then I found a way to ask, without putting my friends on the spot. As a writer for *FiveThirtyEight* (Nate Silver's statistics-minded website), I decided to take advantage of my job to learn more about how other people felt about public acts of prayer or personal moments of prayer in mixed-faith groups. I pitched to my editor the idea of using our survey tools to explore people's reactions to witnessing prayer.[2]

I asked about a wide range of acts of public religiosity: saying grace before meals, talking about your religion, asking others about theirs, praying in public without involving others, asking others to pray with you, marching through the streets in a procession, and so forth. For

[2] Leah Libresco, "When Does Praying in Public Make Others Uncomfortable?", *FiveThirtyEight*, September 16, 2016, https://fivethirtyeight.com /features/when-does-praying-in-public-make-others-uncomfortable/.

each possible activity, I asked Christians how uncomfortable they *thought* these practices made non-Christians. To check their assumptions, I also asked non-Christians (with an emphasis on atheists and agnostics) how uncomfortable they felt when they witnessed these acts of public piety.

For some questions, the atheists' and Christians' answers matched—it's not too hard to guess that most people don't like being asked point-blank about their religious faith. But other questions revealed that Christians underestimated or overestimated how uncomfortable certain kinds of praying can make non-Christians.

Christians tended to underestimate how uncomfortable atheists and agnostics would be if asked, "Would you like to pray together?" A little over 40 percent of the Christians I surveyed guessed that non-Christians would feel "extremely comfortable" or "very comfortable" with this request. Fewer than 20 percent of Christians anticipated that the non-Christians would feel "not so comfortable" or "not at all comfortable". After all, the Christians may have thought, the person they were speaking to could always simply say no and change the topic.

Boy, were they wrong! Sixty percent of atheists and agnostics said that they were "not so comfortable" or "not at all comfortable" with being asked if they would like to pray together. Fewer than 20 percent of these nonbelievers said they would feel "extremely" or "very comfortable" in response to an invitation to prayer.

Although the Christian may (as I did) honestly intend the invitation to be easy to decline, the atheist being asked may not know the asker's heart. The situation becomes tense because the atheist isn't sure what will happen after he says, "No, I'd rather not." Will the next step be a harangue? Will the atheist, having declined an invitation to pray *with*, suddenly find himself being prayed *over*? It doesn't feel as easy to decline without incident as "May I get you some water?" would be.

And when it came to grace before meals, the survey didn't quite solve my problem. About a quarter (27 percent) of atheists and agnostics felt uncomfortable with prayer before meals. Some of that may be discomfort with prayer, period, but, when I interviewed David Silverman, the president of American Atheists, he said his answer to my question would depend a lot on the way I was saying grace. Asking everyone at the table to join hands or bow their heads left him feeling backed into a corner. He wouldn't be able neutrally to avoid participating, and he didn't want to endorse tacitly a faith he opposed. He told me that he would prefer the Christians in the room to pray quietly and independently, to avoid turning the beginning of the meal into a sudden straw poll of "Who here believes in God?"

Exposing this kind of division felt more acrimonious to him than almost any other kind of difference that could exist between the guests. A Super Bowl party with fans from both teams (kitted out in their team's colors) might get heated, but there's no implication that people on the other side thought you were getting an important moral question terribly wrong. That threat of judgment and rejection left Silverman a little uncomfortable even with my usual practice: saying grace audibly, but quietly, and without recruiting the whole table to join me.

What was the point, he wondered, of my praying aloud? If I was trying to thank God, didn't I think that God could hear me perfectly well if I prayed with my thoughts? Anything I bothered to say aloud felt less as though I was aiming it at God and more as though I was targeting it at him and any other nonbelieving guests. We were in a tricky spot. He felt excluded if I prayed in front of him, and I felt

I was excluding him when I didn't! I should be as reluctant to hold back from sharing the good of prayer as from sharing the good things to eat that were on my table.

Witness without Winces

My survey data covered people in the aggregate and suggested that it might really be difficult to begin praying before meals in a group of strangers. But I seldom eat with strangers; I usually eat with friends, family, or both. I have the chance to talk about why I pray *before* the plates hit the table. Some of the acts of public prayer that made my survey takers uncomfortable might be things I'll avoid, but others, such as grace before meals, are things I might find a way to keep doing. I just want to make sure that crossing myself at the table isn't my friends' first exposure to my faith. I want to make space for them to ask me about prayer beforehand, so they have the chance to find out that I'm not thinking contemptuously of them, as David Silverman and pre-conversion-me believed.

My survey data also revealed that some prayer practices were received as unobjectionable, but many Christians did not anticipate that. These nervous Christians made my mistake. Fearful of giving offense, we lost a number of opportunities to pray. Almost a quarter (23 percent) of Christians assumed that non-Christians would be uncomfortable if they saw us praying with a physical object (such as a rosary or a crucifix), but only 12 percent of atheists or agnostics felt perturbed by it. Christians also misjudged how awkward it would be to decline food for religious reasons (e.g., not eating meat on Fridays). Fifteen percent of Christians worried that this might cause offense, but only 5 percent of atheists or agnostics were bothered by it—the lowest figure for any of the examples I asked about.

Many of these more palatable prayer practices involve nothing stronger than an implicit invitation to prayer. Passersby are welcome to keep walking, but they have the option to join in, if they wish. Another way of offering an implicit invitation is not just to pray in public but to do almost *anything* in public visibly as a Christian.

Eamon Duffy argues that abstaining from meat on Fridays, abrogated in the United States to a chosen, private discipline (except during Lent), served and could serve again as that kind of witness. Duffy argues, "By making fasting and abstinence optional, the Church forfeited one of its most eloquent prophetic signs. There is a world of difference between a private devotional gesture, the action of the specially pious, and the prophetic witness of the whole community—the matter of fact witness, repeated week by week, that to be Christian is to stand among the needy."[3]

Through fasting, prayer, or any other kind of visible witness, lay Christians have the chance to offer the kind of mute testimony of the habited religious. In our public peculiarities, we open a door to someone who might not see a priest or nun that day.

The Dominican friars of Washington, D.C., always visible in their white habits, offered a kind of accidental witness during the January 2017 Women's March. Tens of thousands of protesters gathered in the nation's capital. They swamped the subways and spilled out past the boundaries of the official march route. One group of women wandered well south of the National Mall, looking for bathrooms, and walked past the Dominican priory.

[3] Eamon Duffy, "To Fast Again", *First Things* (March 2005), https://www.firstthings.com/article/2005/03/to-fast-again.

The friars threw open their doors, initially to a dozen or so women, but soon a line of more than a hundred stretched out in front of their church. Brother Martin Davis, one of the friars, reflected on the experience after the fact. "Many [of the women] were also fascinated by religious life and the habit we wear. The peculiar situation of some people wearing 'Get your rosaries off my ovaries' next to men actually wearing rosaries on their belts did not stop many from inquiring into what brings us to live lives dedicated to Christ."[4]

Brother Martin and his fellow friars answered women's questions about their vocations, the Church's teaching on abortion, the preferential option for the poor, and other topics. Grateful for refuge, the women spontaneously passed a hat to collect an offering for the church and gave more than a hundred dollars. They handed the sum to Brother Martin, warning him to avert his eyes from the text printed on the hat that they had been passing.

I was delighted by Brother Martin's story, but not too surprised. One of his brother Dominicans had played an important role in my conversion in similar circumstances. I had been attending a panel on science and religion and heard a friar ask the presenters a good question. I buttonholed him at the reception that followed, figuring it was his job to help me out, and he did. Father Dominic (Brother Dominic at the time) offered to have a book club with me to talk about the faith and ultimately was an altar server at my baptism.

When I met Father Dominic, and when the Women's March attendees met Brother Martin, the friars weren't

[4] Br. Martin Davis, O.P., "St. Agnes and the Women's March", *Dominicana*, February 3, 2017, https://www.dominicanajournal.org/st-agnes-and-the-womens-march/.

engaging in traditional witness. They weren't preaching or participating in a street prayer vigil. They were simply being generous while being visibly Catholic.

Offering a Chance for "Amen"

St. Paul Street Evangelization offers another way to be visibly Catholic. The grassroots group sets up tables or signs on busy sidewalks and hands out rosaries to passersby who want them. Anyone who accepts a rosary is also asked if he would like to pray a Rosary, or maybe just a decade, with one of the St. Paul volunteers. The group provides their volunteers with materials and training to make them comfortable in offering apologetics and answering common questions about the faith. The group tries to give fallen-away Catholics and non-Catholics who are curious about the Church an invitation that they can accept.

The next time I have a prayer mixtape event, like my litany-of-saints picnic, I might think about how to open it to outsiders. The first time our group shared saint stories together, we were in public, but not very visible—just one more knot of people on the big lawn of the park. We stood out most when we prayed the litany at the end, chanting, "Pray for us." Next time, I might bring a little sign with "Litany-of-Saints Picnic—Drop-Ins Welcome!" so that people walking by have an invitation to respond to, if they would like.

There's something I would like to add to the Rosaries I pray in public. When I attended World Youth Day in Kraków, Poland, I was delighted to find take-a-prayer, leave-a-prayer stations set up alongside the long lines to enter some of the historical churches. Visitors could write down a prayer intention to leave there, and draw out another pilgrim's. I got to know a stranger through the small intimacy of his most urgent need, and I entrusted mine to someone else.

When I came back to the United States, and my husband and I temporarily took over New York City's Theology on Tap program, we brought a similar prayer box to the pub, and we took home any intentions left over. My husband and I read the intentions and prayed for each one. It broke up some of the flatness of a big crowd for me—I was awed at the pain and love present in the group, even though I didn't know *who* had written a particular intention.

Sometime soon, when the weather is nice, I think I'll get the box out again and take it to the park for anyone who would like to drop an intention in (or pray for one of mine). Whether I'm approached by fellow Catholics or anyone else who simply hasn't had a reason to pray that day, I would like to be able to interrupt their day and mine to care for each other. Once a stranger or a friend has offered a small amen, what other gifts of God might they be willing to say yes to?

8

Home as a Center of Gravity

When I tried to be hospitable—to extend invitations that my friends could say yes to—I defaulted to planning events. I invited people over to *do* something, whether it was to discuss an article, to apply for jobs, or to sing. These specific events seemed to be more attractive than less-structured gatherings; they were experiences you could miss out on. When I pictured less structured events, I thought of cocktail hours and other similar events I had attended. At these events, there was still a busyness—people circulated in and out of conversations—but it seemed like a flurry of activity directed at nothing. My events were the alternative: activity directed toward a sensible goal.

I didn't imagine another option beyond these two models, until I picked up *Bed and Board: Plain Talk about Marriage*, by Robert Farrar Capon, an Episcopalian priest. In one passage, Capon's description of hospitality pulled me up short, even if he was describing the relationship between a mother and a child, not a hostess and her guests. Capon told mothers:

> You are not only a link with something. You are the *thing* itself; and you are the sacrament, the instrument, by which we learn to love the things that are. Your body is the first object any child of man ever wanted. Therefore, dispose yourself to be loved, to be wanted, to be available.

Be *there* for them with a vengeance. Be a gracious, bend-
ing woman. Incline your ear, your hands, your heart to
them. Be found warm and comfortable, and disposed
to affection. Be ready to be done by and to welcome their
casual effusions with something better than preoccupation
and indifference. It isn't a matter of how much time; only
how much intensity. Children love fat mothers. They like
them because while any mother is a diagram of *place*, a
picture of *home*, a fat one is a clearer diagram, a greater
sacrament. She is more *there*.[1]

I didn't feel at all like a fat mother to my friends, even
though I often opened my home and baked cookies to
boot. I never assumed that thereness was all that was wanted
in the events I hosted. I invited my friends to debates,
play readings, and a birthday party that was a doubleheader
screening of Stephen Sondheim's musicals *Company* and
Passion, followed by a symposium on the nature of love.
I was an eccentric professor, or an intellectual ringmaster,
but not so much a picture of home.

I was leery of simply *being* with friends, however much
I liked them. Even when I had less structured time with
closer friends, it was almost always scheduled, not spontaneous. When I looked around for a better example of
what Capon's fat motherhood could consist of, the exem-
plars in my circle weren't mothers, weren't women, and
weren't Christian.

Two friends of mine shared a two-bedroom apartment
and opened their house every weekend for board games.
Their game days were a standing commitment—a reliable
thereness to come home to. Whereas my events had start
times listed on the invitation, and stragglers risked disrupt-
ing our movie or debate or other activity, the boys were

---

[1] Robert Farrar Capon, *Bed and Board: Plain Talk about Marriage* (New York:
Pocket Books, 1970), 49.

able to welcome people who drifted in and out. Their apartment became a home outside home, one of sociologist Ray Oldenburg's "third places", the places required for friendship to grow and flourish.

Hospitality away from Home

Third places are gathering places that come after the first (home) and second (work) places where people spend their time. Oldenburg argues that a casual gathering place is the third leg of a tripod. All three legs are needed to support human life and human society. Third places have a campfire-like quality—they are spaces for leisure and fellowship.

Oldenburg lists several key characteristics of these places. They are neutral ground; they are levelers—open to the public and welcoming to a diverse range of people. The primary activity in these spaces is conversation (not as in most modern coffee shops, where many patrons are quietly working on laptops). They are bustling and full of people—a patron of a third place never worries that it won't be worth stopping by or that there will be no one to talk to. Third places can keep this promise because they attract large groups of regulars. Ideally, a third place is close to the homes and workplaces of its patrons, so it is easy to drop in.

Many of these criteria can and should describe a parish church. But there are a number of logistical difficulties that make it hard for modern American churches to be welcoming in this way. Some churches do not have the staff to keep their doors unlocked at odd hours. Parishes in a city may serve one set of parishioners during the week (those who work nearby) and another set on weekends (those who live nearby) and have trouble becoming a home to either group.

A church also does not exist primarily to facilitate conversation (except with God). A sanctuary should not become the kind of boisterous gathering point that Oldenburg praises (Hannah's passionate prayer in the book of Samuel excepted). A parish would need to open an additional room, perhaps in the rectory with a perpetual coffeepot, to offer a place for people to become friends with other churchgoers.

Although a bar might be the beating heart of a neighborhood, third places cannot be the center of a Christian community. They are light, pleasant places—chosen in a way that the first two places, home and work, are not. They are not usually places for mourning with those who mourn or confiding a long-held fear. But they can be the place to meet and to begin loving those who will weep and pray with us, in the intimacy of our homes or before the tabernacle, once our friendship has blossomed.

A home can be a bridge between the more casual, convivial third place and the intimacy of a home kept by one of Capon's fat mothers. At a broader BenOp event, my home is sometimes much more like a pub—a noisy, cheerful place full of friends or about-to-be friends. We may be puzzling over big ideas, but the intimacies are fewer: we're more likely to bring up something we've read than a wound in our lives. When I have a close friend or a few friends over for dinner, we can share more of ourselves, both the light joys and the deeper sorrows. My home can be a third place for the initial visits, until my guest and I grow to love each other, and then we open up other rooms of our hearts to each other.

But, in our earliest meetings, when I want to cultivate the seeds of a friendship, the most plausible, semithird place to invite a friend is usually the nearest coffee shop. Unfortunately, these stores fall short of the fellowship of a neighborhood place. Seldom am I or my friend a regular wherever we go; neither of us is inviting the other into a place we love. We are not offering a small intimacy.

In a commercial establishment, neither my friend nor I is offering hospitality; we're both consuming it. The store takes on the responsibility of taking care of us. I don't have to be attentive to my friend's minor discomforts or needs—the barista will be the one to offer directions to the bathroom and to wash our cups when we finish.

Companies work to blur the line between guest and customer, to step further into the role of the host. *New York Times* restaurant reviewer Pete Wells balked at Union Square Cafe's style of referring to the people who eat there as "guests" not "customers". In his review, Wells praised the servers for their attentiveness, but he didn't want to misconstrue their friendliness as friendship. He stuck to the paper's style guide, which specified that anyone who paid for a service was a customer, and only those who did not pay could be guests.

One reader wrote in to complain, asking Wells, "Did your experience at USC feel like a transaction? Your review didn't read as such." Wells agreed that the restaurant made him feel at home and cared for, but he maintained this was artistry, analogizing it to a disappearing act. "Union Square Cafe made the machinery of commerce invisible", he wrote. "That's the trick."[2] A steady diet of such tricks of illusory hospitality would starve us.

Humble Homes away from Home

Both host and guest may long to meet in the warm atmosphere of a home, but shifting an appointment out of a

---

[2] Pete Wells, "What Hospitality Means to Times Restaurant Critic Pete Wells", *New York Times*, May 3, 2017, https://www.nytimes.com/2017/05/03/insider/what-hospitality-means-to-times-restaurant-critic-pete-wells.html.

coffee shop and into a living room can be difficult. It's impossible for a number of my friends casually to invite someone to their homes. They live out in Queens or East Falls Church or another suburb of a major city that requires an hour-long commute or more. For them to invite someone to "get coffee" in their kitchen means asking him to take two hours to get to their home and back (and maybe another hour to get all the way home to his far-flung exurb). It's much simpler to meet after work in the city proper, before you go your separate ways. In the long run, friends can try to move to the same block, or even just along one subway line, to have the chance to be more neighborly. For the present, one compromise might be to look for a plaza or a park in the city, where you and your friends can get away from the hovering servers and be more responsible for serving each other.

But something will still be missing; there are some opportunities that come only with welcoming someone into my house or being welcomed into theirs. When I ask people over, I get to assume responsibility for their well-being, and I also give them a more intimate glimpse into myself. Once we leave behind the pseudo-living room of a coffee shop, my friends look not at trendy wall art but at my bookshelves. A number of my guests share my penchant for walking straight to the shelves, scanning them for books we have in common and exclaiming over favorites. Hospitality is an unveiling, in which my guests show me their needs, and I show them something of what I am.

Inviting people into my home is also an accelerant for storgé, the kind of fondness that grows out of shared circumstances. Moving out of a manicured restaurant or coffee shop puts us at greater risk of the small disasters that turn into "Remember the time you told me that eggs could go into the garbage disposal, but then it broke?" We're more likely to share adventures and to rely on each other.

I've had a much easier time growing to like friends of friends when they come to my house or I go to theirs than when I see them only in bars or similar afterwork get-togethers.

Sarah Grey, a writer and editor, found a way to invite her friends into this kind of intimacy more often and gave me a helpful example of Capon's thereness to crib from. She and her husband, feeling lonely in a neighborhood where neither of them had roots, decided to open their house every Friday. They would make pasta and meatballs and feed as many of their friends as felt like RSVP'ing.

As their initial trial became a successful tradition, they had to make a few changes. They limited the guest list to ten adults and "as many children as can play well together without too much supervision".[3] They never expanded their menu beyond meatballs: the food was their excuse to gather; it didn't need to be fancy, just tasty. And they decided to strike a balance between comfortable mess and beauty: paper napkins, but the good china plates; an untidy house, but candles lighting the table. Grey's Friday Night Meatballs were my inspiration for the First Friday BenOp dinners I hosted in Washington, D.C. I wanted to offer the kind of standing promise she and her husband made (and that my games-hosting friends did, too): here is a place you can come home to. Here is a third place to drop into and see the regulars. Guests might describe the atmosphere as either a third place or a home, depending on the mood of the night, or their own mood and needs when they walked in the door.

This kind of regular, but casual, commitment is what Billy Baker, a reporter for the *Boston Globe*, sought out

[3] Sarah Grey, "Friday Night Meatballs: How to Change Your Life with Pasta", *Serious Eats*, August 2014, http://www.seriouseats.com/2014/08 /simpler-entertaining-friday-night-dinners-end-loneliness-how-to-build -community-after-having-kids.html.

when an editor assigned him a story on why middle-age men seldom spend time with friends. Baker took stock of his own life and realized that he barely saw his own friends, not more than a couple of times a year. When he went looking for men who were more deeply rooted and asked how they did it, he met Ozzy. Ozzy turned down other commitments "because he had 'Wednesday Night' ".[4] The barely named tradition was a promise that he and his friends had made. If they were all in town on Wednesday night, they would get together.

Baker was touched by their humble commitment and wished he had a similar one. He wrote, "Everything about the idea seemed quaint and profound—the name that was a lack of a name (such a guy move); the placement in the middle of the week; the fact that they'd continued it for so long. But most of all, it was the acknowledgment from male friends that they needed their male friends, for no other reason than they just did."[5] The men Baker found have promised not to open their homes but simply to *be* with each other, all other details negotiable. There is no goal beyond experiencing "how good and how pleasant it is for brethren to dwell together in unity!" (Ps 133:1, KJV).

Cultivating Interruptibility

When I went about adapting Sarah Grey's meatball suppers for my BenOp community, our dinners were still primarily about unstructured thereness, but I added prayer.

[4] Billy Baker, "The Biggest Threat Facing Middle-Age Men Isn't Smoking or Obesity. It's Loneliness", *Boston Globe*, March 9, 2017, https://www.bostonglobe.com/magazine/2017/03/09/the-biggest-threat-facing-middle-age-men-isn-smoking-obesity-loneliness/k6saC9FnnHQCUbf5mJ8okL/story.html.
[5] Ibid.

For once, I wasn't yielding to my usual temptation to *do* something, rather than just to *be*. Praying the psalms of Evening and Night Office together was a bit more structured than Grey's open-ended dinner but was still in keeping with the goal to rest in each other's presence. We just added another Presence.

For Christians, it is impossible just to *be* with each other without some space for prayer. Christ tells us that "where two or three are gathered in my name, there am I in the midst of them" (Mt 18:20). Without a structured prayer or a moment of silence or extemporaneous petitions and thanksgiving, we are ignoring the cause of our being. We can't fully see and enjoy each other without seeing who we are, and my being an adopted and beloved daughter of God is much more the core of my identity than the books I've set out on my shelves. To see only the parts of ourselves that are embedded in this world, and to ignore the world to come, is to cut off the most lasting part of who God made us to be.

We also need prayer when we are at rest with each other, to give God the chance to break into the conversation. Father Michael Connors, of the Congregation of Holy Cross at Notre Dame, wrote in a Lenten reflection for his campus community that he wanted to cultivate a readiness to receive the Lord. He wrote, "One of my dearest friends used to have a sign on the outside of his office door. It read, 'O Lord, make me interruptible.' "[6]

Interruptibility, Connors observes, is a kind of hospitality. It is a willingness to be receptive to your guests, to accept and care for them as they are. When I am a host, interruptibility often feels magnanimous—a way of

[6] Father Michael Connors, "Reflection—March 1, 2017", Faith ND, March 1, 2017, http://faith.nd.edu/s/1210/faith/social.aspx?sid=1210&gid=609 &pgid=34836&cid=69047&ecid=69047&crid=0.

generously extending myself. But it's impossible to extend that idea of interruptibility to my relationship with God. I am not interrupting the rest of my life when I turn to God to return His constant attention to me; if anything, the rest of my life is an interruption of my communion with God—the ultimate end we are made for and which the saints in heaven enjoy in the Beatific Vision.

Connors wrote his meditation on interruptibility during Lent, which breaks into our routines and gives us the opportunity to return to God. We break up our usual routines to go to Mass in the middle of the week on Ash Wednesday, to spend three consecutive days in church during the Triduum—the services of Maundy Thursday, Good Friday, and Easter. We return our attention to God and let Him speak to us without having to shout through apparitions or miracles. During the rest of the liturgical year, it is our task to set aside time to unfold our hearts to God and to be with Him in attentive silence.

To know God, I must be interruptible by Him. And, the more I thought about it, the more I wanted to offer some of that sort of attentive interruptibility to my friends as well. Thereness is the art of presence, of being responsive to others, available to be interrupted and returned to the act of seeing and loving each other. Opening the door to spontaneous, unscheduled encounters allows me to reorient myself so that I am more easily moved by love, not my own plans.

Designing Places for Encounter

Mike Lanza is one of the most ingenious architects of encounter I know, even though he wasn't motivated by theological reasoning. Lanza wanted his children to grow up as part of a neighborhood community, but he knew that modern suburbs don't facilitate the same sort of spontaneous friendships throughout the block that he had grown up with. When no children play outside, the emptiness of the street becomes self-perpetuating. All the virtues of front stoops as third places—places where you can expect to find regulars—are lost. Some family has to take the initiative to be out and visibly available for play, or everyone will stick to scheduled playdates and miss out on child-initiated spontaneous play.

Lanza decided that he and his family would change the social life of their neighborhood. To attract other children as playmates for his kids, he turned his front yard into a third place for children. Instead of a tightly trimmed lawn giving off a "Don't mess me up" vibe, he filled his front yard with an all-weather whiteboard, a picnic table, a sandbox, a fountain, and more. Every time he added an element, he thought carefully about what would make it most inviting to children. The fountain he designed was one that "children could play with safely. It has no standing water, no sharp edges, and a very low profile—about 16 inches off the ground. It's extremely popular with toddlers and dogs passing our house, so it acts as a 'gateway' to families into the rest of our yard."[7]

I would like to set up a similar hub of children's play when my husband and I have kids and a home we're allowed to alter. But in the meantime, Lanza's advice helps me to think about how to make my home and my events inviting, so that friends want to wander in and share part of their day with me and anyone else who has stopped by. For Lanza, it all starts with accessibility. "If neighbors and passers-by can't get to your yard, they won't hang

[7] Mike Lanza, *Playborhood: Turn Your Neighborhood into a Place for Play* (Menlo Park: Free Play Press, 2012), 32.

out there", he writes. "All barriers limit accessibility, but some do so more than others. A barrier with a gate is a lot more accessible than one without a gate. A barrier with an opening rather than a gate is even better.... At my house, we try to keep the gate to the backyard open at all times, and we also offer a ladder to kids who want to hop our backyard fence."[8]

I can't physically open up my home as Lanza does: I don't own the front door of my apartment building. But I can lower nonphysical barriers. Some of the obstacles are logistical: Am I scheduling at a time that works for friends with heavy work schedules? Am I providing good food and enough of it?

But there are spiritual barriers as well. My own sin or my friend's fears can build walls between us. If I have trouble praying the Litany of Humility, struggling to say, "That others may be esteemed more than I, Jesus, grant me the grace to desire it. That, in the opinion of the world, others may increase and I may decrease, Jesus, grant me the grace to desire it", I've put up a barrier between me and God, and thus between me and His creation. If I struggle to pray as I ought but reach out to a spiritual director or a friend for help or even simply turn to God and say, "I don't know how to mean this litany when I pray it; please teach me", then I've put a gate into that barrier.

To invite others in, I need to open not just my home but also my heart. I must learn from God how to offer myself. In my life, this offering is more often in moment-to-moment presence than in a single moment of sacrifice. Hospitality is training to welcome others, to receive their welcome, and to anticipate the kingdom of God. Father Henri Nouwen, who spent much of his life sharing thereness with the profoundly disabled of the L'Arche community, saw the work of welcome as part of our inheritance as children of God.

In one of his books, Nouwen explores Rembrandt's portrait of the return of the prodigal son. Nouwen shares his meditations on the way he resembles both the erring and repenting prodigal and the obedient but stiff-necked elder brother. He explores the love of the father for them both, and the love of God, our Father, for us all. In the final pages, having imagined himself in the role of both children, he dares to think of how he might be called to cleave to the father as well, not just in an embrace, but by being transfigured by love to be him. Nouwen writes:

> The closer I come to home the clearer becomes the realization that there is a call beyond the call to return. It is the call to become the Father who welcomes home and calls for a celebration.... When I first saw Rembrandt's *Prodigal Son*, I could never have dreamt that becoming the repentant son was only a step on the way to becoming the welcoming father. I see now that the hands that forgive, console, heal, and offer a festive meal must become my own.[9]

The patient father that Nouwen glimpses in Rembrandt and the squashy, waiting mother envisioned by Capon are icons of God's love. When I ask God to make me more like Him, when I ask Him to let me rely on Him in my friends, I learn who He is.

[9] Henri J.M. Nouwen, *The Return of the Prodigal Son: A Story of Homecoming* (New York: Image Books, 1992), 119.

9

Welcoming the Stranger

You can plan community events with the best of intentions, but you may still wind up feeling like the king in the parable of the wedding banquet, who sent out invitations that were not accepted. As you and your friends work to thicken your Christian community, you'll have to find ways to bring people in, not just to fill out your ranks, but to share whatever good things you're making with others who long for them. But adding people is more than just getting them to show up.

Ben Kuhn, a friend of mine who is active in the Effective Altruism community, thinks hard about how to make new people feel welcome in his community. One piece of Ben's advice applies to BenOp hosts as well: "Figure out how their perspective can add to [the community], not what [the community] should subtract from them."[1] If I don't have a sense of what a new person can add, I probably want a better introduction to him, so I can know and love him better. I can't introduce a new person generically to my BenOp friends: "Jane, this is our vibrant community. Community, this is Jane—who is one additional person!"

[1] Ben Kuhn, "On Being Welcoming", *BenKuhn.net* (blog), May 2015, http://www.benkuhn.net/welcoming.

Breaking Up Cliques, Making Newcomers Welcome

When someone comes to my home for the first time, I have a couple of approaches to try to let him see and be seen by the friends I already know well. The first intervention is the most quotidian: I ask the guests at most of my events to wear name tags. It's more than a little self-serving: I'm pretty face-blind (to the point where I realized an hour into my very first date that I was out with a different person from the boy I thought had asked me out!). Putting a pile of name tags and a Sharpie by the door saves me a lot of embarrassment. But I think it also helps my guests. It's easier to pick up a conversation with someone you've met only once before if you're not afraid to approach him because you've forgotten his name. A new attendee won't be the only person at sea in a room full of people who know each other. And it's easier (for me, at least) to feel connected to a person when I can see his name and connect it to him throughout our conversation, instead of struggling to hold on to it at its first and only mention. I don't care how dorky people say name tags are; I would rather look a little silly than not have a clue as to what my new friend's name is by the end of our first meeting.

But name tags aren't enough. They help me and my friends with continuing a conversation, but they don't give us a reason to talk to a stranger in the first place. I wanted ways to make the individuality of my guests as immediately visible as their names. I needed a better icebreaker than the traditional "Where do you live? What do you do?"

The introductory question I've settled on is "What's something interesting that you've recently read?" When

I'm hosting, before our official start, I usually have attendees go around in a circle and give their names and their answers to the question. People name novels, scientific papers, history books on a niche topic, a piece of investigative journalism, and, usually, as we go around the circle, there are frequent interjections. "I *loved* that book!" "Wait! Can you repeat the author's name so I can write it down?" "If you liked *that*, you should read *this* next!"

Asking people to share something that they loved gave us all a reason to be interested in the people around us, including anyone who was a stranger. Each new guest has the chance to be seen and welcomed as particularly himself, not just as a thin outline of a person. Often, someone in the group wants to buttonhole the new guest, either immediately or later in the event, to keep talking about the topic or book they discovered they had in common.

There are other icebreakers of this type you can invent for your circle. The most important thing about my question is that it's an invitation to share something beloved. When guests tell us about something they love, we have the chance to see them as they are: people made to love (and also to be loved by God). It's easiest for me to kindle love for a new acquaintance when I see him in love with someone or something.

Almost everyone in my circle of friends has something to say in response to my prompt about reading, but, depending on what moves your community, you might ask about music, prayers, art, experiences of nature, or acts of kindness. Anything works, as long as it moves us to wonder and delight. It's even a gift to use such a prompt in a group of people who know each other well and may not seem to need such an intimate kind of introduction. On many social media platforms, we endlessly reintroduce ourselves by sharing what we hate or oppose—sometimes to mobilize others to action, sometimes simply to vent.

This habit gives me a horrendously distorted portrait of my friends and acquaintances. I see them most truly when I see what they would fight for, not against.

Creating Fellowship through Shared Experiences

Another approach I take to breaking up cliques and making room for new people is planning events around a shared experience. At an unstructured event, there's a temptation to continue previous conversations and make inside jokes with the people you already know well. As new people drift in and out of conversations, it can be hard to notice them or to care for them. In these circumstances, I can miss opportunities for fellowship, and I can actively turn away from others in a way that may be sinful.

In Pope Francis' *Open Mind, Faithful Heart*, a book adapted from his lectures for priests on pastoral care, he discusses what the sin of lukewarmness, the fault for which God says He will spit us out of His mouth (see Rev 3:16), looks like within a friendship. Pope Francis writes:

> When dealing with strangers, we are surprised to encounter strong emotions, whether hatred or gratitude, but with friends it is different. We feel stunned when they are only lukewarm toward us. That is the great sin against friendship. A lukewarm attitude conceals the opportunistic types, those "eternally perplexed" persons who are always wondering whether to commit themselves or not. They are forever waiting as they make their precise calculations.[2]

I recognized myself in those last two lines. At some general meet-and-greet events, I find myself asking vague

[2] Jorge Mario Bergoglio, *Open Mind, Faithful Heart: Reflections on Following Jesus* (New York: Crossroad, 2015), 209.

questions ("Oh, when did you move there?"), simply to move the conversation along, with no real interest in the questions I'm asking. In the moment, it feels like I'm being polite: the new person hasn't caught my interest, but I'm not being so rude as to walk away. My middle ground is offering the illusion of a conversation. I offer my nothings ("Did you stay dry this weekend during the storm?") to volley my side of the conversation back and patiently wait out the other's replies.

Since I have trouble leaping into intimacy but also have trouble making it through small talk, I like to get to know others by offering a meaty, shared experience. The simplest event of this kind is a movie night. When I invite people over to watch *A Man for All Seasons* or *Of Gods and Men* or *Les Innocentes* (all good films for a BenOp group, though the last two are harrowing), we spend most of the event in silence, watching the film. Once the credits roll, our conversation has a natural direction: we all want to discuss the film. In the ensuing conversation, the new people are on an equal footing with old friends; we're starting from a fully shared experience.

At these events, I'm often drawn into a back-and-forth with someone I've never met. Before knowing each other's names, we are discussing our views on martyrdom and our relationships with some of the saints.

Another way to give your guests a shared experience is to have prereading for an event. The traditional option is to host a book club, but I think your friends' previous bad experience in book clubs (no one reads the book, the event drifts to general socializing) may leave them unlikely to make a commitment to yours. I prefer to shape my events around shorter readings. I might choose a chapter of a nonfiction book, two paired essays, or a long-form piece of journalism—something my friends could start and finish on the day of the event, if necessary. Now, instead of spending the majority of the event watching a movie, we have the chance to jump in immediately and share our thoughts.

The simplest way of creating a shared topic is just by picking a shared topic. My first Benedict Option gathering was just a dinner for people who wanted to discuss the Benedict Option. I had suggested some prereadings, but none were required. Everyone simply brought their hopes and doubts and set to it. After my husband and I married, we began attending a monthly meet-up of young Catholic couples (both married and engaged), during which all the attendees shared challenges or joys they had encountered in their lives together. In another setting, a friend of mine (a non-Christian) organized a day of conversation about how to cultivate "Hufflepuff Virtues", by which he meant the kinds of virtues that are humble, focused on service, seldom labeled "badass". He thought his Silicon Valley social circle underappreciated these virtues (and, as a result, seldom got to enjoy their fruits), so he had a symposium to talk about why they might be valuable and how his community could inculcate and celebrate these traits.

Any shared project or question can become the focus of an event. I always feel excited about making one of these events someone's first exposure to my friends, as we all pitch in together. I like to set aside the last half hour or so of these events to talk about concrete actions we might take as a result—with a focus on things we might do in the next week or the next month, so that the enthusiasm we've built up doesn't dissipate.

Deepening a Casual Get-Together

Another way to invite strangers in (or to persuade them to invite you in) may be to find a way of adding intimacy to an

existing event. When I lived in D.C., my parish had a coffee hour after Mass. Moments before, we had shared the
greatest intimacy as we received Christ's Body and Blood
in the Eucharist, but now we could shore up the smaller
intimacies, such as learning each other's names. Our parish
gave us the space to meet each other, but we didn't always
give ourselves permission to approach each other. People
tended to drift toward those whom they already knew.

The one group of people I found it natural to strike up
a conversation with (for a pretty broad definition of "conversation") were the small children crawling across the
floor and the toddlers knocking pell-mell into my knees
just as I filled a coffee cup. After a round of making faces
or playing peekaboo with a tiny child, I would eventually
get around to asking the baby's parents what their child's
name was, what their own names were, and possibly more.
It took a different ministry to help me make friends with
people who were unaccompanied by children.

After coffee hour, our parish offered adult Sunday
school, taught by the two Dominican friars attached to our
parish. They joined us as part of their preparation for the
priesthood, each spending one year as an altar server and
then one year as a deacon. Once our friars were ordained,
they celebrated their first Masses at our parish, before being
sent into the world on assignment. As part of their service,
they taught anywhere from fifteen to thirty-five parishioners every Sunday in a small classroom. The class topics
were chosen by the friars (we could submit requests) and
covered anything from an introduction to Vatican bureau-
cracy, to the theology of annulments, to a book club on
Sheldon Vanauken's *A Severe Mercy*.

We were encouraged to break in with questions and
comments, so, in addition to learning about the faith, I
also learned about my classmates. Even if it took me a little

while to learn someone's name (sadly, there were no name tags), the question someone asked or a moment of grace a person shared in conversation stayed vividly with me. The adult Sunday school was the most age-diverse group I have ever belonged to. We had retirees sitting alongside summer interns. Come Christmas, I happily accepted the invitation of one of the elderly couples to their caroling party, which took me to a suburban neighborhood I had never visited. Several years later, I lectored at the wedding of one of the older women, who had met her husband at an event outside the parish that she had attended with me.

The adult Sunday school wasn't gimmicky, trying to use something unrelated to the faith to get us in the door. It was a lot more fun and intimate than the wine-and-cheese-and-small-talk events for young adults I had also tried out. The class brought us together to consider our faith and let us reveal our genuine needs in the questions we asked.

The only thing I wanted to add was a coda. I wish we had had the room for just an extra half hour after the class wrapped up. After an hour of learning together (or more than an hour, when Brother Dominic was the teacher), I wanted to rest in the company of the other attendees. I wanted the space that the parish's coffee hour had tried to set aside, but at a time when I was already introduced to and engaged with others. I tried to imagine what would give us the option to stay.

The best idea I came up with was pretty similar to the coffee hour: I considered bringing cookies to eat *after* the event. If someone wanted to grab a cookie and head out, that would be okay; they weren't meant as a bribe. But they would give anyone who wanted to stay an excuse to do so. ("I'm staying to eat this cookie" sounds more reasonable than "I'm just staying", however odd it is to need an excuse for fellowship). I never made this happen at parish events while I lived in the city, but I changed the way I planned some social events with this in mind. I started bringing out a light dessert or snack when the "official" part of the gathering ended.

When New People Spark New Conflicts

Welcoming strangers and strengthening connections between acquaintances is usually a blessing. But sometimes expanding your circle comes with growing pains. You may find that you don't know how to welcome everyone at once, if some of your guests are uncomfortable around others. I almost gave up going to my parish's coffee hour after a man there pressured me for my phone number repeatedly. When he moved *during Mass* to sit closer to me, I thought I might have to switch Mass times or parishes entirely. (Eventually his attentiveness faded.) I never went to my priest for help, because I didn't know what he could do to help me—the Mass is the source and summit of our life; how could the parish *not* welcome the man who was scaring me?

I didn't have an easier time with this kind of problem when it happened in my own home, even though I *can* bar people from my living room without affecting their access to the sacraments. Some of the men who came to my BenOp dinners made *me* uncomfortable, though I never knew whether they were oblivious or obnoxious. Eventually, one of the women who frequently came to my events said she wanted to start RSVP'ing to me over e-mail, privately, rather than on Facebook. When I asked her why, she told me that one of the men who had been my guest was making her uncomfortable, and he seemed to be using her RSVPs to make sure he would be there when she was. (She had already, unbeknownst to me, been skipping any events that he RSVP'd to first.)

She didn't want to give me his name; she didn't want me to confront or ban him. So all I could do was accept her private RSVPs and try to be attentive to her conversation. (I never figured out who the culprit was.) I could make food and set out chairs, but, as a host, I felt powerless to take care of my guests in the face of harassment. Women are more likely than men to be on the receiving end on this kind of behavior (and to feel frightened, not just frustrated), but in any social space, at church or at home, there may be someone who has trouble coexisting in that space with others. Hospitality is taking care of others, and if I have people over to my house, feed them, show them where the bathroom is, and so forth, but don't take care of them by protecting women (or anyone else) from harassment, my guests can't be at home in my house.

Houseguests can also make other guests uncomfortable without engaging in sexual harassment. A friend of mine had a problem with a woman in his small church group who had a bluntness that bled into insult and a disregard for others' personal space. It was hard to tell whether the behavior was deliberate or a social impairment. In these circumstances, it's hard to figure out how to be fair to everyone involved.

In college, one approach I saw hosts take was to post people by the door, keeping an eye out for any women who weren't quite leaving under their own power. They weren't running tribunals on consent, but they were trying to make it harder for anyone to prey on their attendees or innocently to make a serious mistake.

I don't throw the kind of events that allow people to get that inebriated, but I try to take turns around the room and break up conversations that someone seems to have trouble getting out of. And I keep an eye on the exits. At events when everyone is leaving in a group, I've tried to squelch my impulse to get everyone out in one sweep. Someone hanging back to help clean up or to use the bathroom may be deliberately lingering to avoid leaving in the company of another guest.

Another possible approach, if your problem attendee might not be aware he's disruptive (and isn't fixated on one person who would be a target for retribution) is to speak to him directly. Treat his difficult behavior as a problem for *him* as well as for others, since it's pushing away other attendees. I'm not qualified to diagnose the root cause of a social problem, but I can say that certain behavior doesn't work in my spaces, and that I'm happy to talk about what help my guest might need to be able to stick to the norms I've set up. Does he have trouble recognizing the boundaries others need? Would it help to have someone act as minder with a hand signal or a quiet cue to back off? Are the events stressful in some way, and would it be easier to take breaks or step outside, as some of my introverted friends do?

If you offer community to people who are hungry for it, some of the people who turn up will be those who struggle to find friends due to external constraints (a recent move, a busy job, etc.), and some will be those who washed out of other communities because they had trouble sharing space with others. As much as you can, it's good to avoid turning people away on account of their hunger and to pray for help in offering the works of mercy to shelter the homeless and fraternally correct the erring.

But it might take some time before you're prepared for the fraternal part of fraternal correction. I'm more conservative when I make initial connections with a group, so that bad experiences don't break us up before we have the chance to become brotherly. I want to be able to reach out to a problem guest affectionately and for him already to know me as more than the keeper of the rules. It's hard to ask someone to ask for my help if we barely know each other. If you build your initial community on a foundation of trust and amity, you'll be better able later to rely on each other to welcome people who are difficult.

The one constant option is prayer. The intercession of Our Lady, Undoer of Knots, chaplets of Divine Mercy, or petitions to Blessed Pier Giorgio Frassati (who brought his friends together for Rosary hikes, among his ministries) may be helpful. If possible, try to pray with people on both sides of the conflict, either separately or together. Don't be afraid to ask God for miracles. He is the One I trust to break stony hearts, including my own, if I am being too cautious or fearful. Invite Him to do so!

Getting Others to Invite Themselves into Your Life

When I am feeling tangled up in interpersonal tensions, I try to keep in mind what kind of community I'm trying to create. In the long term, I pray that we may all be saints in heaven, but, in the short term, as often as possible, I am often trying just to help people find each other, and to fall in agape love, the love that resembles God's love for us. The process is turbulent, but, since it's what we are made for, it's not too hard to have faith.

When I need encouragement, I like to remember the small miracles of Via Fondazza. This Italian street changed its character when one of the residents posted fliers announcing that he had created a closed Facebook group for everyone on the block, and he hoped people would join. Today, about half the residents of Via Fondazza belong to the group, and they use it to ask small favors of their neighbors.

One of my favorite anecdotes about the street comes from an article by *New York Times* reporter Gaia Pianigiani, who revealed the intense competition between neighbors to solve a plumbing problem. Pianigiani laid out the sequence of events: "Caterina Salvadori, a screenwriter and filmmaker who moved to Via Fondazza last March, posted on Facebook that her sink was clogged. Within five minutes, she said, she had three different messages. One neighbor offered a plunger, then another a more efficient plunger, and a third offered to unblock the sink himself. The last bidder won."[3]

The street was transformed by transparency. When the neighbors had easy ways to share their troubles or to offer something of themselves, the dams opened. I had been part of a similarly electrified community when some Catholic bloggers who all contributed to the same site formed a small group. Originally, we meant to share tips on how to navigate the formatting of our blog network, deal with ads, and negotiate with management. Quickly, without anyone specifically organizing it, our Facebook group was full of prayer requests. I knew the deepest pains of these bloggers better than I knew my neighbors' or even many of my friends'. And to this day, I have never met in person many of these people, with whom I've shared some private needs.

[3] Gaia Pianigiani, "Italian Neighbors Build a Social Network, First Online, Then Off", *New York Times*, August 24, 2015, https://www.nytimes.com /2015/08/25/world/europe/italian-neighbors-build-their-own-social-network -online-and-off.html.

In my own neighborhoods, I've never belonged to anything like the Via Fondazza community. Although some buildings I've lived in offered e-bulletin boards, they were hosted on our building's portal, which I, like everyone else, logged on to only once a month to pay rent. You couldn't post something like "I have cookies in the oven, come to apartment 701 in thirty minutes to eat them!" and expect anyone would see it in time. A literal bulletin board in the elevator would have worked better, since people would have had a fighting chance to see it. I hesitated to make this suggestion in my next apartment building, which was so opposed to clutter that residents were forbidden to put anything on their doors, and delivery boys were not allowed past the lobby, lest they hang menus in the hallways.

Despite those hurdles, I've twice gotten to welcome people whom I wasn't seeking out. In New York, I was required to let the doorman know if I had more than two people coming over, so he would know to send them up. I usually let him know what my husband and I were hosting when I tipped him off. After I asked him to let people in for two Shakespeare-related events in short succession, he wanted to know if he could introduce my husband and me to another resident, who he knew was a Shakespeare buff. She joined us for our reading of *Julius Caesar* on the Ides of March, and we kept her on our list for future events.

In D.C., my apartment didn't have a doorman-matchmaker, but it did have access to a spacious roof. When the weather was nice, my friends and I held our monthly debates up there; we were the odd ducks with our gavel and our parliamentary procedure among other residents who were sharing wine or swimming. As I was setting up for one of our debates, a woman came over with her twelve-year-old son in tow and asked, "Are you the group that debates on the roof?" I said yes, slightly worried that she was frustrated with us. But, instead, she asked if we would let her son sit within earshot, since he had overheard one of our previous debates and enjoyed it.

I told her that would be impossible, but we would be very happy to have him sit *with* us and to participate as well. From that day until his family moved out of our building, the boy came to all of our debates (without his mother) and was made much of by everyone who attended. He asked questions and gave speeches; he was smart, curious, and also happened to be the only person his age most of us interacted with.

We met our Shakespeare friend and our debater because we were visible, even if we weren't *as* visible as the people on Via Fondazza had become to each other. But each of these meetings was a narrow miss: if we had kept the debates in our apartment, if I hadn't chatted up the doorman, the people who found us would have passed us by. There must have been more people in those large buildings who would have enjoyed being included, if only they had also found a way to be invited. And who knows what we might have been welcomed to in other people's homes?

Bridging the Gaps

When I try to reach out to other Christians, I ask myself, "What would it take for *me* to reach out to a stranger?" I want to make sure I'm extending an invitation that is recognizable as such. When I pray the Rosary in a public place, it feels as though I'm being publicly Catholic enough to be approached, but when I imagine myself as an observer, I realize that I would never strike up a conversation with someone just because I saw that he was praying. The most I would do would be to smile or nod. I have to extend myself further, until I've offered at least the kind of invitation that I myself would accept (and since I'm pretty extroverted, I might want to go a little further still).

The other rule of thumb I've found helpful is: How much am I relying on God to work miracles to make an introduction? I'm surrounded by Christians. I see proof of it every Ash Wednesday, when suddenly the streets are full of people with ashy crosses or when I've discovered that a co-worker is Catholic—we've just never mentioned our faith to each other. This day of fasting always uncovers a secret abundance. If I want to make contact the rest of the year, I need to do more than wait for a booming voice to introduce us, or a subtler form of God's serendipity.

When Pope Francis visited the United States, all the usual discretion was suspended. Catholics overran the streets, and even outside the official events, there was a kind of visibility and festive atmosphere that made me want to take chances and be generous. One night, in New York City, I was giving directions to a group of young out-of-towners taking a late-night train to Philadelphia. I figured they must be trying to see the pope in the last city of his tour and were probably Catholic. I asked them if that's where they were headed, and when they said yes, I asked them something I would usually ask a stranger only if he was a habited religious: "Would you like to pray a Hail Mary with me while you wait for your train?"

I would love to receive the blessing of shared prayer in more ordinary times. I want to encounter strangers, even with all the bumps and bothers that come with them, and have people walk into my life and teach me to love more generously. The people I would not have sought out, who find me serendipitously or who are brought as a friend of a friend, who often manage not quite to fit in are the ones who help my friends and me to grow.

Those in a spiritually healthy Benedict Option group shouldn't be surprised to find that they don't all mesh perfectly. And someone who requires a few adjustments on your part in order for you to welcome him might offer a chance to discover something new that your group would like to try. It may turn out that it's not only the new arrival who would like to have more gatherings focused on silent prayer; the new person is just the first to admit to wanting more. As C. S. Lewis writes in *Mere Christianity*, "Sameness is to be found most among the most 'natural' men, not among those who surrender to Christ. How monotonously alike all the great tyrants and conquerors have been, how gloriously different are the saints."[4] We shouldn't suppress ourselves to fit into a group. If a group of friends experience too much pressure to conform and converge, they will be less likely to grow into the "gloriously different" saints that God intends them to be.

Christians gathered together for worship may find themselves praising God like the blind men exploring the elephant. One person is touched by God's tenderness, another by His majesty, another by His beauty, still another by His simplicity. In our shared, varied worship, we are a little like a living psalmody, sounding the range of loves we creatures offer in response to the one, perfect love our Creator offers us.

[4] C. S. Lewis, *The Complete C. S. Lewis Signature Classics* (New York: HarperOne, 2002), 176.

10

"She Looks Well to the Ways
of Her Household"
(A Cheat Sheet of Logistics)

When you invite into your home friends and strangers who aren't friends yet, there are habits you can cultivate to make it easier to welcome them as an act of love, rather than as a mad scramble that leaves you strained and anxious. Here are some of my tools for scheduling events, sharing them, and setting up my home that have made a big difference in the way I offer hospitality, both to BenOp friends and to others. I hope they can serve as a cheat sheet for the events you and your friends plan, smoothing your way as you welcome each other.

One of my day jobs required me to prepare convivial spaces. I was responsible for organizing retreats for my co-workers every three months. Everyone at my company worked remotely, so we got to see each other only at these week-long gatherings. As the company grew, I planned events for twenty-five people, then thirty, then forty, with an attendant increase in complexity each time. One of my co-workers, trying to give me a compliment, asked me how I managed to make the retreats run smoothly. I answered, a little too honestly, "I just imagine you all are slightly tipsy, slightly petulant toddlers, and then I make plans that will work despite that handicap."

I could stand to be more tactful, but the fact remains that it helps me run BenOp and other events when I idiot-proof them as much as possible and remember that I'm not just taking care of the guests. It helps to compensate for my own moments of tipsy, petulant toddlerhood, too. During one work event, we split into small groups for dinner in different restaurants. I assigned people to groups, made the reservations, and then typed a list of everyone's groups, the restaurant, the address, and the time it would take to drive or walk there from our hotel. I gave everyone everything they needed.

Then I thought about the whole plan from the tipsy, petulant perspective and realized how much work I had still left for my co-workers, whom I was ostensibly taking care of (consult the list, contact everyone in their group to decide when they'd leave, etc.). I kept the omnibus list as a failsafe, but I started making separate calendar events for each dinner group, so people could see only the information that was relevant to them. And I named every event the same way: Dinner at [restaurant name], X-minute walk, Y-minute drive.

It wasn't too hard to figure out what else my co-workers might need. I just imagined them not arriving on time for their dinners and then thought about what could plausibly have gone wrong. I make my own plans using the same kind of thinking. When I put events or reminders on my calendar, I try to write the note as though I know I'm going to be hit very hard over the head right before the appointment, and I'll have to reconstruct my plans from my calendar notes alone. As a result, I started making sure I saved addresses, not just the name of where we were meeting. I copied and pasted information from the e-mails I had received about the appointment, rather than assuming I could look those details up while I was on my way.

After all, I would have to piece together all this information at some point. All I was deciding was whether I would do it ahead of time, in a moment of relative calmness, or whether I would delegate it to my future self, the one hustling to get to the event on time. I can't know what spirit I'll be in just before my commitment: I might have had a bad day or be miserably rushing. Preparing in a moment of peace is a way of being hospitable to myself.

I'm still trying to move past the defensive mind-set of "tipsy, petulant toddlers" so I can do this planning as an act of love. Instead of thinking of my friends (or myself) as incompetent, I can think about smoothing the way for them, as in making "the crooked straight and the rough places plain" (Is 40:4).[1] My temptation is to think of my preparations as indulging the foibles and deficiencies of my guests, rather than taking their needs seriously. Readying the event for them is no more condescending and no less loving than getting a glass of ice water ready for a guest on a hot day. These are some of the small logistical adjustments that have helped me welcome others, starting before they arrive at my house.

Picking a Date

I rely on a tool called Doodle.com to pick dates for any event I host. The website lets me select a list of dates and times and then send out a virtual sign-up board to all the friends I plan to invite. They check off the dates when they're available and x out the times when they're busy. Within a day or two (maybe prodding one or two laggards), I can easily see which date will work for my over-committed friends.

[1] George Frideric Handel, "Every Valley Shall Be Exalted", *Messiah*.

In the absence of a scheduling tool—whether Doodle or some other online survey program—picking a date can be one of the most exhausting parts of planning. And it leaves the guests and the hosts feeling a little aggravated, rather than anticipatory. E-mailing a group to ask about their availability means that everyone's first experience of the event is a string of e-mails such as "I can do Wednesday until 9p" and "Can we change the Thursday time to be 5p, not 7? Can everyone reply again about the new time?"

It's much nicer for guests to reply only once, so that there's nothing to blunt their enthusiasm about the invitation. It's also a big help to me as the host, since the responses are all automatically tabulated. I also get a sense of whether people are interested; I've canceled some events when I've floated the idea and then noticed that everyone was suspiciously uninterested in filling out the Doodle about dates. Finally, because the respondents know that they helped choose the date, they may have a greater sense of ownership of the event and want to make sure they keep the date free, once I make the final call.

Inviting the Guests

Once I've chosen a time, I tend to use Facebook to send invitations. Almost any service can work: an invitation-focused service such as Paperless Post, a calendar event you share, a simple e-mail reminder, or cards written in calligraphy (if that's what you want). But Facebook has worked particularly well for me for these reasons.

Reminders are built into the service

Before I began dating my husband, I had tried online dating, and I was stood up for two or three dates in a row. I figured I had to be doing something wrong, and when

I asked my friends, they figured out the problem: I had scheduled the dates three weeks in advance (I was busy!), and I hadn't sent a reminder to the guys the day before the date to make sure we were still on. I was aggrieved. I had put the date on my calendar right when we had scheduled it—what were the men doing?

I still don't know what was up with those guys, but I've become convinced that many folks don't have a calendar, a datebook, or another system that reliably helps them to keep their appointments. If folks are still working with a hodgepodge of Post-it notes, memory, or who knows what, I want to send my invite knowing I'm plugged into *some* system that they use. Facebook hits the mark for me, since I know it will prompt them with reminders on the day of the event. Depending on what your friends use, there may be a better service for making sure that they don't miss your event by mistake.

*The event page is a natural place to share things
with other guests*

A Facebook event includes a wall—a forum for posts by the host and the guests. That makes it easy for anyone coming to the event to share links to articles, photos, videos, or anything else we think would be of interest to the people attending. The shared message board functions as an ephemeral and unobtrusive listserv. The posts are easier to ignore than an e-mail chain, but guests can jump into the discussion if they're interested. For those participating, the chance to bounce ideas or recommendations off others stokes enthusiasm for the event.

I've had friends use the event page to ask questions about the logistics of the gathering and to share suggested prereading for a discussion. After the event has ended, there's often a flurry of posts, as people follow up on conversations that started at my house, sharing a promised book recommendation or even a link to another upcoming event. I like that having a way to follow up with this particular group of people gives us all a way to keep caring for each other after the event.

If the gathering touches on a sensitive topic, I'm more likely to make the event private (so noninvitees can't see the posts that are written), but for innocuous events, I leave the whole thing set to "public". Thus, I tend to set movie nights as public, but a discussion about abortion (with both pro-choice and pro-life folks attending) I set as private.

It's easy to invite others

Bringing in more guests isn't a selling point if what you're planning is a quiet dinner party for you and five friends. For small events, whose guest lists are limited by necessity or design, I would be more likely to rely on a simple e-mail invitation (with a reminder the day before). But, for a lot of the events I host, it's a double bonus if guests invite their friends. They enliven an event such as a hymn sing or fill out the cast of a play reading. But, more than that, it's likely that I would enjoy meeting the kinds of people who enjoy coming to the unusual events I host. Someone who takes up a friend's invitation to a Fourth of July party is probably simply interested in a general spirit of celebration. Someone who wants to discuss *Laurus*, a Russian novel about a holy fool, is more likely to be someone I want to meet.

Making the Food

It's always an option to buy food, whether you get take-out for the group or pick up something premade earlier in the day. When it comes to cooking for a crowd, I've had the best luck with casseroles or cold food, both of which don't leave me tense about timing. I really like making the cooking part of my hosting plan, because I get to take care of my friends in a very corporeal way, and I get to give them something good, something I really like myself (never make a recipe you don't enjoy eating yourself!). When I choose recipes for groups, I read them with an eye for the following red flags:

The recipe is either good or bad—it doesn't fail gracefully

Here are some dishes I will never make for groups: soufflés, emulsions (mayo, hollandaise sauce, etc.), or a custard that never thickens up. I want to make foods that in the worst case will go only a little wrong—slightly too soft, a little burnt. But I don't want to make anything that might fail a critical step completely, as when a soufflé falls. I read recipes carefully, looking for wiggle room and making sure there's no step that says anything like "overstir just a little, and it will be ruined." My friends can eat slightly botched food, but not food that never quite turns into food at all.

There's a frenzy of work at the end—and then the dish must be served immediately

I don't mind having some cooking work left to do as people arrive, but I don't want to be in the middle of the hardest step, right when I have to keep opening the door and greeting people. Not everything can be a casserole, which I can make ahead of time, put it in to bake, and then have only to take it out of the oven, but it's best if I'm only idly stirring or waiting to flip something, instead of concentrating hard and waving people off.

One or more steps take a lot longer if
I double the recipe

At big events, I usually double or triple the recipe I make. And at one event, I got myself into big trouble with a spring-squash pasta bake. It's a casserole bake, so I figured I was all set: I would make three dishes of it the night before and then just heat them up the next day. Making three times as much pasta was easy; it all fit into my giant pot. Chopping the three times as much cheese and herbs and squash took a bit longer but was still manageable.

Then I hit the problem step: I had to sear all the squash slices, putting each slice in the pan, undisturbed, for ten minutes. With three pounds of thinly sliced squash on my hands, even with pans on two burners, it took me till well past my bedtime. Now I'm very careful to avoid culinary choke points, moments when I need to interact with an ingredient piece by piece. And I watch out for doublings that will mean I can't fit what I'm cooking into one pot or one pan anymore, and what was once a single roasting, searing, or sautéing step will now be a cycle of repeating the step again and again. I still really like that pasta bake,[2] but I save it for small events.

My basic approach to big meals is to serve people starch, with something interesting in it: pasta with walnuts, gorgonzola, roasted tomatoes, and wilted arugula; farro with roasted squash, feta, and mint; a different pasta with mushrooms and marsala. As long as you pick one fairly interesting thing to mix in, everyone will be happy. And the base starch will stretch your more fun ingredients. (It will stretch them even further if you have time to dump one

[2] Deb Perelman, "Herbed Summer Squash Pasta Bake", *Smitten Kitchen* (blog), June 22, 2015, https://smittenkitchen.com/2015/06/herbed-summer -squash-pasta-bake/.

more box of pasta into the boiling water, as I've done when more people turned up on short notice.) Cheap and delicious aren't mutually exclusive.

When it comes to dessert, I like to try out more elaborate cookies or cakes, but one of the most reliable options is to premake cookie dough and rest it in the fridge so that you can bake it and serve it fresh from the oven. Or, for medium-size groups, I like to make a skillet cookie[3] (exactly what it sounds like—a skillet-size cookie) during the event and then serve it to general delight. People love seeing it come together.

Setting Up the Room

One of the simplest parts of setup was to make the welcome-to-my-house announcement, where I pointed out the bathrooms and let people know it was all right to use my bedroom as a second room during the event. The room I offered in D.C. was not much bigger than a walk-in closet and had no windows or overhead lights, and it was mostly occupied by my bed. But I made sure to tidy up and offer the space, since I never knew when someone might want to attend my event but not always be present at it.

The second room was for mothers who wanted to nurse their babies in private (or for anyone who wanted to withdraw if a mom preferred to nurse in the main room). A parent could take an overstimulated child there to calm down, a guest could take a call privately, or an introverted

---

[3] sophistimom (Jaime), "One-Pan Dark Chocolate Chunk Skillet Cookie", *Tasty Kitchen* (blog), February 16, 2011, http://tastykitchen.com/recipes/desserts/one-pan-dark-chocolate-chunk-skillet-cookie/.

guest could take a break from the hubbub, with or without a friend. The main virtue of a second room is that it allows you to have more than one atmosphere or energy level at a party. It's hard to design an event to suit everyone; offering a second, flexible space helps guests to take care of themselves.

If all you have is a bedroom, as I did, it can be a big help to open it up. (If you're worried about tidying, I recommend putting everything you've left on the floor in a cardboard box and leaving it there during the party—you can dump it back on the floor at the end of the night.) In practice, although I tried to steer people to the bedroom, the real second space in my apartment was the kitchen. Folks drifted in, seeking a second space for conversations, even in my New York City apartment, where the kitchen was cramped enough for any cooking I was doing to present a real threat to guests.

When it was harder to split the space, I tried to think about ways to make more time for quiet at events. I wanted to be better able to welcome introverts and to have more space for contentment, rather than excitement. The most obvious tactic I could come up with was food: you can talk only so much with your mouth full. Food, particularly food made and presented with detectable care (rather than snacks or takeout pizza), prompts quiet, attentive eating. Kate Donovan, the blogger behind *Gruntled and Hinged*, suggests a few other ideas for welcoming introverts, including centering an event on a physical activity. She likes to have introverted-but-social time at a trampoline gym or playing ping-pong, in which the fast pace of play makes sustained conversations implausible. Or, if she's looking to have shorter breaks in a more conventional event, she likes to have things for people to do with their hands, so that taking a moment's pause (to knit, to adjust a puzzle piece, etc.) is par for the course.[4]

One of my favorite pieces of advice about organizing the room came from Rabbi Kaunfer's guide to supporting independent minyanim (Jewish prayer groups). Kaunfer has an eye for detail and even has something to say about offering hospitality by crowding your guests (in a nice way). He writes, "At a movie, you might hope the theater isn't crowded and there is enough breathing room around your seat. In a synagogue service, by contrast, there is value in feeling a bit crowded."[5]

Kaunfer wants to push people together, because the groups he leads sing their prayers, and he wants people to be close enough to hear their neighbors and blend their voices. Spread out across the room, his guests might be singing together, technically, but each person's prayers can't be shaped by hearing each other's song.

I could sympathize. At most parishes I've visited, the parishioners spread themselves out across the pews as if trying to achieve an exactly even spacing, only a few people per pew, everyone careful not to sit directly behind anyone else. It's impossible to pass the peace except as a half-hearted wave, and all the hymns sound thin and lonely.

At my events, there was never enough space for that sort of problem to persist, but I wanted to make my room feel lively. In inviting twenty or thirty people over, how could I help the first five or ten arrivers to avoid rattling around? Kaunfer had the answer: "At Hadar, we always put out

<hr />

[4] Kate Donovan, "Pugs in Boots, Introverts, Social Interaction", *Gruntled and Hinged* (blog), February 10, 2015, https://gruntledandhinged.com/2015/02/10/1590/.

[5] Elie Kaunfer, *Empowered Judaism: What Independent Minyanim Can Teach Us about Building Vibrant Jewish Communities* (Woodstock: Jewish Lights, 2010), Kindle edition, location 1993.

fewer chairs than necessary in the beginning, so people will be drawn to sitting near others. Only in the middle of the service, when people are packed in, do we add more chairs."[6] I start nights by directing people to the couches and the armchairs. As more people arrive, I have them grab folding chairs from my closet, adding them just where they need them to join a conversation.

To build up a thick community of Christians, it can help to make the events feel cozily crowded. Picking a date that works for many people, sharing the details so that they can make it to the event, taking care of food for everyone, and organizing the room to be pleasantly busy (with an escape for those who need more space) is how I try to gather us together in Christ's name. All the logistics and planning is meant to prepare a space, to clear away distractions so that we can hear God more clearly and respond to His love.

[6] Ibid, location 2016.

I I

Returning to God

When I tried to come up with plans and strategies to form stronger Christian communities, I cribbed ideas from everyone: cooking bloggers, urban Jews, California transhumanists. The desire for community isn't limited to Christians, so it's possible to find good ideas nearly everywhere. But the pervasiveness of these kinds of projects poses a question: What, if anything, makes the Benedict Option specifically Christian? What distinguishes it from community building (as done by Christians)?

Christians and Christian projects have always attracted this kind of question. What is the difference between being a Christian and just being a nice person, a generous person? In a letter to Diognetus, written sometime in the second century A.D., a Christian named Mathetes observes:

> Christians are indistinguishable from other men either by nationality, language or customs. They do not inhabit separate cities of their own, or speak a strange dialect, or follow some outlandish way of life. Their teaching is not based upon reveries inspired by the curiosity of men. Unlike some other people, they champion no purely human doctrine. With regard to dress, food, and manner of life in general, they follow the customs of whatever

city they happen to be living in, whether it is Greek or foreign.[1]

But for all this, we don't just blend in, or at least we shouldn't. Mathetes goes on to say:

> And yet there is something extraordinary about their lives. They live in their own countries as though they were only passing through. They play their full role as citizens, but labor under all the disabilities of aliens. Any country can be their homeland, but for them their homeland, wherever it may be, is a foreign country. Like others, they marry and have children, but they do not expose them. They share their meals, but not their wives. They live in the flesh, but they are not governed by the desires of the flesh. They pass their days upon earth, but they are citizens of heaven.[2]

We sing songs together, we break bread, we spill out into the streets in processions all because we live in hope, longing to find our home in heaven with our Lord. Too often today, people know our faith primarily by its list of "thou shalt nots", but they should be able to see in our lives some reflection of the One we have said yes to. Sometimes, the simple fact of our joy is a countercultural witness. It can help someone who couldn't otherwise imagine giving up whatever is standing between him and the Church: sleeping in on Sunday mornings; feeling solely responsible for his strengths; having premarital sex. Or at least he couldn't imagine giving those things up and feeling hale, happy, and whole as a result of the renunciation.

[1] *Epistle of Mathetes to Diognetus* 5, quoted in "The Christian in the World", Vatican website, http://www.vatican.va/spirit/documents/spirit_20010522 _diogneto_en.html.
[2] Ibid.

We Christians have the chance to make it imaginable, by living our faith in public.

Among ourselves, we must also keep in mind what we say amen to and resist the temptation to define our faith in an oppositional way. The Benedict Option is not primarily a retreat but is meant to help us draw closer to Christ, so that we can receive His grace and allow it to spill out through us. When people worry about or endorse retreat, all I can think of is Claudia Kincaid's snappy rejoinder to her brother Jaime when he questions her plans to run away from home (and live in the Metropolitan Museum of Art) in *From the Mixed-Up Files of Mrs. Basil E. Frankweiler*:

> "Of all the sissy ways to run away and of all the sissy places to run away to ..." Jaime mumbled.
> He didn't mumble quite softly enough. Claudia turned on him, "Run *away* to? How can you run *away* and *to*? What kind of language is that?" Claudia asked.[3]

As Christians, we run *toward* not *away*. We are in the same position as Saint Peter when he said to Christ, "Lord, to whom shall we go? You have the words of eternal life" (Jn 6:68). We are called to run headlong toward God, which means that when we appear to be running *away* from anything else, it's because that thing is not also moving toward God. Some things we flee from are intrinsic evils, but others are lesser goods that we aren't called to reject so much as to restore to the right balance in our lives.

Gathering together to share our faith with others can be a way of running toward God. But, undergirding any Benedict Option community, there should be a commitment

---

[3] E. L. Konigsburg, *From the Mixed-Up Files of Mrs. Basil E. Frankweiler* (New York: Aladdin Paperbacks, 1967), Kindle edition, 25.

to the places God has told us to run to find Him: the sacraments. The seven sacraments are the places God has promised us we will always find Him; although He may dispense His grace at any place and at any time, the sacraments are the gifts He has given us where we know grace is efficacious. The *Catechism of the Catholic Church* (*CCC*) says of the sacraments, "Because they are signs they also instruct. They not only presuppose faith, but by words and objects they also nourish, strengthen, and express it" (1123).[4]

The sacraments we can most easily run toward are confession and the Eucharist. Like the other sacraments, as Saint Thomas Aquinas tells us, each of these operates as a "sign that commemorates what precedes it— Christ's Passion; demonstrates what is accomplished in us through Christ's Passion—grace; and prefigures what that Passion pledges to us—future glory".[5] Unlike the other five sacraments, confession and the Eucharist can be sought in any season of our lives. If we are running away *to*, we will be found not on a hill or in a bunker, but in the confessional, preparing ourselves to receive Christ in the Eucharist.

If we want also to chase God anywhere else, we're in luck, because He's chasing us first. As the psalmist writes:

> Where shall I go from your Spirit?
> Or where shall I flee from your presence?
> If I ascend to heaven, you are there!
> If I make my bed in Sheol, you are there!
> If I take the wings of the morning

---

[4] Quoting Vatican Council II, Constitution on the Sacred Liturgy *Sacrosanctum concilium* (December 4, 1963), no. 59.

[5] *Summa theologica* III, q. 60, a. 3, quoted in *CCC* 1130.

and dwell in the uttermost parts of the sea,
even there your hand shall lead me,
and your right hand shall hold me. (Ps 139:7–10)

Since God is already seeking us, it rarely takes a burst of
activity on our part to reach Him. It's more likely that
we might need to pause for a moment of stillness and
allow Him to overtake us. Robert Cardinal Sarah writes,
"God's only power is to love silently. He is incapable of
any oppressive force. God is love, and love cannot compel,
force, or oppress in order to be loved in return."[6]

The trouble is, I am terrible at silence. I have twice
picked contemplative prayer as a Lenten discipline simply
because I am aware that I can't go on being so dreadful at
it. I struggled to be silent for five minutes at a time, content to rest in God's presence. In prayer, I ask God to make
me more His own, but, in the meantime, to please give
me cruder, louder cues, since I struggle to catch the words
He speaks in silence. I ask Him to sanctify me through the
example of my friends, of His saints, of anyone at all who
can teach me to return His love. I am not fluent in the language of silent love that He made me for, so I ask Him to
teach it to me again, as a second language, using the forms
of beauty and charity I recognize.

Cardinal Sarah reminds us that silent adoration of God
is the prayer we will always have. All other forms of spirituality prepare us to be with God. Contemplation is a spirituality of extremes—it is the consolation we long for in
heaven, but it is also the only kind of prayer left to us
in the depths of misery. Sarah explained in an interview,
"When I traveled to countries that were going through

---

[6] Robert Cardinal Sarah, *The Power of Silence: Against the Dictatorship of Noise*
(San Francisco: Ignatius Press, 2017), 59–60.

violent, profound crises, sufferings and tragic miseries, . . .
I observed that silent prayer is the last treasure of those
who have nothing left. Silence is the last trench where
no one can enter, the one room in which to remain at
peace, the place where suffering for a moment lays down
its weapons."[7]

When I converted to Catholicism, people in my
RCIA class (where I and others seeking to join the
Church learned about the faith) took turns giving a pre-
sentation about a saint. This spiritual show-and-tell was
meant to help us discover holy men and women we
might choose for confirmation saints and to show us the
tremendous range of ways to be holy. By hearing what
God had called forth from others, we might have a better chance of noticing what He might be asking of us.
I chose to present on a saint in whose life silent prayer
was the impregnable redoubt that Cardinal Sarah praised:
Maximilian Kolbe.

Kolbe was a Franciscan priest who died in a Nazi con-
centration camp. His life before the camp was full of
sanctity—he created an international group dedicated to
the Virgin Mary and founded a monastery in Japan—but
I was most moved by the circumstances of his death. He
had been sent to the camp for sheltering Jews and pub-
lishing anti-Nazi tracts, and he gave his life for another
prisoner. To punish prisoners for an escape, the camp
guards chose ten men at random to be starved to death.
One of the condemned men asked for mercy, saying that
he had a wife and children; Kolbe stepped forward to
take his place.

---

[7] "Cardinal Robert Sarah on 'The Strength of Silence' and the Dictatorship of Noise", *Catholic World Report*, October 3, 2016, http://www
.catholicworldreport.com/2016/10/03/cardinal-robert-sarah-on-the-strength
-of-silence-and-the-dictatorship-of-noise/.

I wasn't transfixed only by Kolbe's fearlessness or his generosity. I was dumbfounded by the witness of his joy. Once he and the other nine men were locked in a bunker to starve, Kolbe led his fellow prisoners in prayer and hymns, ministering to them until they died. Kolbe lived far longer than would be expected, and the guards eventually killed him by lethal injection.

In his martyrdom, Kolbe didn't just defy the Nazis; he revealed the emptiness of the power over others that they claimed. They could lock Kolbe up, deny him food, even end his life, but they couldn't take away his will to love others as Christ does. In a place consecrated to killing, he was an icon of love, and the God Who is Love beats all idols hollow. Like Christ trampling down death by death in His Passion, Kolbe immolated the falsity of the Nazis' constructed world.

More recently, Father Douglas Bazi, a Chaldean priest, imitated Father Maximilian Kolbe's indomitable love. Bazi was kidnapped and held captive by Shiite militiamen in Iraq. In an interview with Jonathan Coppage after his release, he explained how he used the very chains of his imprisonment as the means of prayer. Bazi said, "I used to pray by that chain, pray the rosary. With much praying I became calm. I really became stronger, sometimes I was aggressive with them. When they asked me questions, sometimes I was laughing, I asked them, 'What kind of stupid question was that?' Sometimes I felt that they were captured by me, I was not captured by them."[8] Although Bazi was their prisoner, his guards ended up treating him as a spiritual authority, even asking him for advice about how to treat their wives.

---

[8] Jonathan Coppage, "We Know That We Are Going to Be Killed", *First Things*, July 5, 2016, https://www.firstthings.com/web-exclusives/2016/07/we-know-that-we-are-going-to-be-killed.

If Kolbe and Bazi could be channels of God's grace in such circumstances, I know that there is always a way for me to love as Christ does, if only I will ask God's help to do it. So, when I feel thwarted or afraid or tempted to despair, I try to return to the work of love, in whatever small way is readily at hand. After my conversion, one of the first ways I tried to do this was by embracing prayer as a circuit breaker. When I felt the prickling of a grudge, tempted to root my heart in anger, I prayed a Hail Mary. I wasn't even praying *for* the person I was failing to love; I was just praying to give myself a break from hating and to see if, with a little breathing room, I could do something else.

I've tried to take any feeling of fear or hopelessness as a similar spur to prayer and action. To be a Christian means to believe that hopelessness is always a misapprehension at best, and, at worst, a form of spiritual attack. I look for ways to live according to the eschatological hope that led C. S. Lewis to bellow to his friend Sheldon Vanauken, "Christians NEVER say good-bye!"

Usually, faced by small threats, my acts of love as defiance are similarly small. On one occasion, when political developments left me feeling miserable and powerless, I baked cookies for all my friends with young children. I sent the packages off in the mail, saying to myself that, although I wasn't sure what to do about big, national problems, I was hardly lacking opportunities to care for others at the interpersonal level. I might as well do whatever I could *definitely* do and turn to God to reflect further about what else I could offer.

Another time, my husband and I, exhausted by vituperative news cycles, threw a poetry-recitation night at our house. We wanted to make more space for beauty in our lives and the lives of our friends. We chose to make it a *recitation* night, rather than a reading night, requiring our friends to memorize the poems they wanted to share. Our goal was to let all our friends who attended make space for beauty not just in our home but also within themselves. They would need to carve out time to learn (or relearn) the poems they were going to recite, and, as a result, they would walk away from our one-night event still carrying the poem within themselves, holding on to something beautiful that could not be taken from them.

This wasn't one of our BenOp events—we wanted to be able to welcome our non-Christian friends—but for Alexi and me it was animated by the same desire to move closer to the One Who is Beauty, Truth, and Goodness. I chose a Catholic poem to memorize ("Mary Considers the Prophecy of Simeon" by Annabelle Moseley) so that I would be able to carry it within me, just as I carry in my purse a holy card of Mary, Undoer of Knots that my husband gave me. I want to be able to pray through beauty whenever I have the least inclination to. Since I'm not a mystic (at least not yet) that means carrying around icons of God's beauty, whether physically or mentally.

The poetry night was something we could offer to any of our friends, regardless of their beliefs. But although God will always give us something to offer in love, we aren't always able to offer to everyone everything He has given us. Saint Aelred of Rievaulx, an abbot of a Cistercian abbey in the twelfth century, drew a sharp distinction between the love Christians could offer and receive from non-Christians and the friendships they could share among themselves. He wrote, "Divine authority commands that many more be received to the clasp of charity than to the embrace of friendship. By the law of charity we are ordered to welcome into the bosom of love not only our friends but also our enemies. But we call friends only those to whom we have no qualm about entrusting our heart and all its contents."[9]

His teaching sounds harsh, as though we are deliberately withholding the best parts of our love. The first time I read his work, I recoiled at this passage and others like it. But there truly are times when, as a Christian, I am constrained from offering the fullness of my love and wind up offering a translation or a dilution of my initial impulse. I can bring a casserole to anyone who has suffered a loss, and I'm glad to be able do it. But I can't bring the icon of Christ harrowing hell and leading Adam and Eve out of their graves to a nonreligious friend who is grieving. Or, at least, I can't expect that friend to derive comfort from it without an explanation first.

How can I offer the comforts I depend on to friends who will see them as alien at best and confrontational at worst? It may be easier to share the sources of my hope in *my* hardest moments, showing the icon of *Christus Victor* to my friend when *I* am mourning. My friend, trying to be with me in my grief, may find that she has a way to enter into my faith as well. In *her* time of suffering, I will offer her whatever she can accept, which will certainly include casseroles, but might not include shared prayer.

In those circumstances, my love will be limited. Our love as Christians has its fullest expression when we offer it to other Christians, because we don't need to withhold (or offer and have rebuffed) the pillars of our love. Although we cannot always offer it to friends outside the faith, we can hope that when they see it from a distance, when we offer it to each other, they may long to receive the fullness of our love and, eventually, God's.

<hr>

[9] Aelred of Rievaulx, *Spiritual Friendship* (Collegeville, Minn.: Liturgical Press, 2010), Kindle edition, no. 60.

Many kinds of sin and ignorance can be rebuked only by offering a positive witness of the love and freedom that is available to us when we leave these temptations behind. Gathering together in BenOp communities to concentrate our love, to love more fully, allows us to receive that witness and point others toward it. Ronald Knox, an English priest of the early twentieth century, praised Dominicans, and Saint Dominic in particular, for making their lives into icons of this kind. Dominic founded the Order of Preachers, friars known for their intellectual firepower and public preaching. But what Knox singled out for praise was not their role as a bulwark against heretical *ideas* (such as those of the Albigensians) but their ability to rebuke error through the mute witness of their chosen lives.

Knox said in a sermon at St. Dominic's at Haverstock Hill:

> An intellectual heresy can be met by the weapons of the intellect; a moral protest, such as that of the Waldenses, can only be met by a rival moral protest within the Church itself. Just as the tide of the Reformation was stemmed, not merely by polemical writing and preaching, but by the great spiritual renewal which was accomplished throughout Europe by the Saints of the sixteenth century, so three hundred years earlier, it was not only the learning of the Friars, but their poverty, their chastity, the simplicity of their lives and manners, that saved Europe for the faith.[10]

Knox argued in his sermon that the witness of the Dominicans' vows made them more than a simple rebuke to the excesses of the world around them. He praised their "spirit of gaiety which goes with poverty, that openhearted

<hr/>

[10] Ronald Knox, *Captive Flames: On Selected Saints and Christian Heroes* (San Francisco: Ignatius Press, 2001), 54–55.

acceptance of the world which belongs only to those who have learned to despise it."[11] They lived the disciplines of poverty and chastity vibrantly. Their lives were a testimony, allowing people to see, rather than be argued into agreeing, that "his yoke is easy and his burden is light" (see Mt 11:30).

Knox delivered his sermon to an audience partially composed of Third Order Dominicans, laity who have thrown themselves into the Dominican charism of study and preaching, anchored by prayer. These tertiaries stand in the middle place, sustained by the friars who have made a total gift of self to God in their vows, deputized to help carry the fruits of their study and their love to the broader world.

Adopting this kind of life, whether through formal vows to a tertiary order or through informal commitments to Christian friends creating a BenOp community, means living in a Pentecost spirit. The Acts of the Apostles describes how, after the descent of the Holy Spirit, new converts manifested the faith: "They held steadfastly to the apostles' teaching and fellowship, to the breaking of the bread and to the prayers" (2:42). This verse could be the motto of any group trying to deepen fellowship among Christians.

When Christ gave the disciples, and, by extension, all of us, the Holy Spirit, He breathed upon them. The Greek word for both "spirit" and "breath" is *pneuma*, and when we pray, we are part of an act of divine respiration. We must always have the attitude of Saint Paul, who wrote to the Romans, "I long to see you, that I may impart to you some spiritual gift to strengthen you, that is, that we may be mutually encouraged by each other's faith, both yours and mine" (Rom 1:11–12). When we gather together to seek

[11] Ibid., 57.

God, love moves back and forth between us, sometimes in swells of joy, sometimes in eddies of grief, but always testifying to the movement of the Holy Spirit among us.

When Christ appears to John in the book of Revelation, He proclaims, "I am he that liveth, and was dead; and, behold, I am alive for evermore" (1:18, KJV). We who live in Christ must, through our love of each other, offer His glory a lively witness.